NERVES OF STEELE

The Phil Steele Story

Llyfrgelloedd Caerdydd
www.caerdydd.gov.uk/llyfrgelloedd
Cardiff Libraries
www.cardiff.gov.uk/libraries

Rn

D0279195

'In the early 1980s when Welsh rugby was not exactly overflowing with gifted players, I went to cover a match at Rodney Parade where one player that that caught my eye was an unknown young full-back named Phil Steele, he was a breath of fresh air.

Since those days, he has developed to become a star in his own right. He is a brilliant communicator whether behind the microphone as a broadcaster, after-dinner speaker (sometimes with guitar at hand) or compère. He also uses his talent to contribute much to charitable causes.

He is a gifted all-rounder and Phil Steele would always be in my side – on or off the field.'

Barry John
Wales – British & Irish Lions

'Phil is a big part of Welsh rugby. His familiar face and voice on television and radio is a staple diet of rugby reporting today. Phil is extremely popular with all the players – and a very funny man!'

Sam Warburton
Wales – British & Irish Lions

'My time with Scrum V was great fun, not least because of the numerous trips with 'Steeley'. Aside from being a terrific broadcaster, away from the camera he's a compulsive raconteur and a constant source of amusement with a black belt in self-deprecation.

Most importantly perhaps, for those that value our downtime, he's always 'got an hour' in him at the end of a shift and is truly one of life's good guys.'

Stuart Davies
Wales

NERVES OF STEELE

The Phil Steele Story

Phil Steele
with
Anthony Bunko

St David's Press
Cardiff

Published in Wales by St. David's Press, an imprint of

Ashley Drake Publishing Ltd
PO Box 733
Cardiff
CF14 7ZY

www.st-davids-press.wales

First Impression – 2016

ISBN
978-1-902719-50-4

© Ashley Drake Publishing Ltd 2016
Text © Phil Steele & Anthony Bunko 2016

The right of Phil Steele and Anthony Bunko to be identified as the authors of this work has been asserted in accordance with the Copyright Design and Patents Act of 1988.

All rights reserved. No part of this publication may be reproduced, stored in a retrieval system, or transmitted, in any form or by any means without the prior permission of the publishers.

British Library Cataloguing-in-Publication Data.
A CIP catalogue for this book is available from the British Library.

Typeset by Replika Press Pvt Ltd, India
Printed by Akcent Media, Czech Republic

Contents

To Liz and Kate,
for loving me and believing in me.

Foreword

There's a well-known and often used phrase among lovers of the oval ball game – that of being 'a good rugby man.'

Being such a man entails not only being a passionate champion of rugby but also someone who espouses the values so integral to the game – those of sportsmanship, respect, fun and friendship.

Phil Steele is the epitome of a 'good rugby man', as anyone who knows him or has spent any time in his company will testify.

Despite the fact that the late, great former Llanelli, Wales and Lions centre Ray Gravell used to jocularly remark, "Phil Steele...not a bad full back.....not a good one either!" Phil was in fact an accomplished player even though one of his clubs did happen to be Newport rather than one of mine, Cardiff!

Phil's rugby pedigree goes much deeper than that of just a player however.

Having been steeped in the game since he was eight-years-old he is a living encyclopaedia of rugby knowledge and a student of the game and its exponents.

But it's the way that he exudes the sheer joy of the game and its characters that really sets Phil Steele apart. His commentaries, reports and interviews for BBC Wales Sport, which are always infused with his trademark humour and affable good grace, never fail to amuse as well as inform and as such have cemented his status as one of the nation's most popular broadcasters.

Similarly, anyone fortunate enough to have listened to him

delivering one of his, always hilarious, after-dinner speeches will realise that Phil has a special ability, as a natural raconteur and communicator, to relate to people of all ages, interests and backgrounds.

It's on a human and personal level that Phil connects best. He is the same in the company of the great and good of the sporting and business communities of Wales as he is with a rugby club Under-8s team or with the most gnarled, old, valleys prop forward.

Deeply caring and compassionate, Phil's support for the Welsh Rugby Charitable Trust, the only charity in Wales which deals solely with helping severely injured rugby players, is something for which I, and my fellow Trustees, am extremely grateful. It's a side of him which few people get to see because it rarely attracts public attention – and it's something about which he is uncharacteristically modest – so I will say it for him.

More remarkable still is that Phil has become this person against a background of a battle against personal tragedy and quite severe mental health issues.

He has overcome these in the way he always approaches life; with a laugh, a smile, and above all an overwhelming urge to enjoy life to the full.

Read on – you'll see what I mean!

Dennis Gethin
President, Welsh Rugby Union
Chairman, Welsh Rugby Charitable Trust

Acknowledgements

Writing your life story is a much more difficult task that I first imagined. I am also now aware that weaving together the various threads of my personal life, the teaching and speaking careers as well as my rugby exploits and battles with depression and anxiety, into a coherent and readable book would have been almost impossible without the aid of Anthony Bunko. He is a very skilled listener and communicator, which together with his easy and gentle manner, meant that we were able to enjoy a great rapport from the outset. This has enabled me to put into words and make public some aspects of my life that I have only previously shared with very few people. Cheers Bunko, you're a top bloke!

I'd also like to offer my grateful thanks to Ashley Drake of St. David's Press for giving me the opportunity to put my story into print.

I'm also indebted to Chris Kirwan of the *South Wales Argus*, Ben Evans of The Huw Evans Picture Agency and BBC Wales for the photographs provided.

I would also like to thank Dennis Gethin for kindly providing the foreword, and Barry John, Sam Warburton, Stuart Davies, Warren Gatland, Alan Wilkins, Huw Thomas, Jonathan Davies, Lee Byrne, Gareth Charles, Richard Thomas, Stuart Davis, Nicky Piper, Carolyn Hitt, Dr. Clive Norling, Mike 'Spikey' Watkins and Eddie Butler for their kind testimonials.

Finally, I wish to thank my legs for supporting me for all these years, my arms for always being at my side and my fingers – as I've always been able to count on them!

Phil Steele
September 2016

'Phil is a likeable and funny person who always enjoys his work and you can see that when he's on TV or speaking in public. He loves life and is great company.'

Jonathan Davies
Wales (Rugby Union)
Wales – Great Britain (Rugby League)

'It's never entirely clear if the entertainer is outwitting a serious character, or if a serious mind is keeping the jester at bay. Whichever, the inner duel makes Phil Steele seriously good fun and a wonderful story-teller.'

Eddie Butler
Wales - British & Irish Lions

1

Plaster of Paris – and Panic

I've been lucky enough to get to know Phil during my time as Wales coach. He is an excellent broadcaster who genuinely wants Wales and Welsh players to excel and I respect his friendly and personal approach. I also admire the fact that he has been able to do this while facing personal and life-changing challenges.

Warren Gatland
Coach: Ireland – Wales – British & Irish Lions

I sat in the darkness of my bedroom. My eyes fixed on the fresh, pristine white plaster of Paris wrapped around my right leg. I knew exactly how I had done it. An injury in the seventh minute of added time while playing for Newport RFC against my old club, Glamorgan Wanderers. Trust my luck. I had been having a reasonably good game as well. If I remember correctly, I think I even made a tackle – one of the three tackles I usually made per season. I was what they called, in rugby circles, a pacifist, non-tackling, full-back!

It had been an enjoyable match. We were winning 25 – 4, on their patch. Of course, I had to put up with the usual cutting Welsh banter from the home supporters.

'Steeley – put a cap on mun, the glare from yer head is

blinding us!' And 'Steeley – you can't still be playing at your age!'

I was used to all that. It came with the territory. Something I'd lived with for most of my life. Even at the tender age of 18 I looked as old as many of my team-mates' fathers. Now I was 23 and I looked as old as some of their grandfathers.

However, on that damp afternoon, as the minutes ticked away, I couldn't wait for the final whistle to sound so I could have a few beers and a catch up with old friends in the clubhouse. Then disaster struck. I'd been tackled and as I was getting up from the ruck, I heard a soft tearing noise. At first, to be honest, I thought the gusset of my shorts had split but, as I tried to get up to jog back into position, I looked down at my right knee. It just dangled there, as if it didn't belong to me and I immediately fell to the ground. I felt no real pain, but I knew something wasn't right. To rub salt into the wound, seconds later the final whistle sounded and the ground emptied, leaving me alone on the cold, muddy turf with only the trainer and the club's doctor for company. I imagined how a wounded soldier may have felt, lying injured on a deserted battlefield.

"I think it's your knee ligaments," the doctor muttered.

I placed my head in my hands and thought, 'Oh no...not again!'

The rugby injury had occurred on Saturday 24th October 1984 – a date which even after all these years is still indelibly imprinted in my brain. Two nights later, as I lay in bed, I couldn't work out why it throbbed so much. The plaster mould seemed to be gripping tighter around the flesh; squeezing it just like a giant python strangling the life out of its victim.

The pain was so intense, I could hardly catch my breath. I knew right then it had to come off. I didn't care what would happen to my leg. I didn't care if it wouldn't knit back together properly. I began to pull at the cast; tearing at it with my bare hands. It wouldn't budge. Even in the darkness I could see my leg turning blue. I was really struggling with the cast now, my entire body bathed in a cold sweat.

"Get off...get off," I yelled.

A nurse appeared from nowhere, holding a sharp pair of scissors. "Don't worry Mister Steele...it will be ok." She said, trying to calm me down.

"Get it off me, nurse...quick...its killing me."

She cut away at the cast but nothing happened. There wasn't even a mark on it. She tried again, putting more force behind it. It just got tighter, as if it had a mind of its own and was determined to do the opposite of what I wanted. Other people now appeared behind her. It was like a scene from the film, *Airplane*. One man held a kitchen knife whilst another gripped a large lump hammer and a schoolboy waited at the back, clutching a chainsaw.

Anxiety gripped me in a headlock and wouldn't let me go.

What was happening to me?

What was going on?

The man with the lump hammer moved the nurse out of the way, before taking an almighty swing.

BOOSH!

The hammer smashed into the plaster of Paris but, yet again, nothing happened, not even a dent. He kept swinging and bashing away. I closed my eyes. I could feel every hit bruising my flesh.

I let out an almighty scream.

Suddenly my eyes shot open. Everything fell quiet. I lay in my bed, all alone, my blankets piled up on the bedroom floor. I breathed a sigh of relief. It had all been a dream, or more like a nightmare. The injury and the plaster of Paris were definitely real. The nurse, and the other people by the bed hitting me with strange objects, thankfully weren't.

I sat there in the dark, my heart pounding as wildly as the drumbeat of a thrash metal band. A wave of anxiety seemed to seep through the wall and engulf me – like a big, black, heavy, all-enveloping cloud pressing on me and pinning me to the bed. I wanted to get up. Panic spread through my body. I needed to see my parents. I needed to feel their safety around me.

Once, when I was really young I got lost in a supermarket. I guess a lot of children would have just raced to the sweet aisle and got stuck in. Not me. I panicked. I remember that feeling as concerned strangers tried to comfort me. I didn't want their help. I wanted the safety of my mother. I ran up and down the aisles until I found her, or she found me.

Now for some reason I felt the same way; lost! This time lost in my own bedroom in my parent's house. I needed to find the safety of my mother again!

Soaked in sweat, I hobbled across the landing to my parent's bedroom. If I had been seven or eight that would have been acceptable. However, since I was 23, it must have appeared a little odd. As soon as I saw them, I felt better.

I didn't climb in between them and *cwtch* up for the night, if that's what you're thinking. Now that would have been bizarre. A six foot three rugby player, scrunched up in between his parents! No, I simply limped back to bed.

I hardly slept that night, as I anxiously tossed and turned, and when I woke the next morning around 9am, I not only felt knackered, I sensed something had happened to me. I had changed. I don't know why! I felt anxious, as if my entire body had automatically switched into constant panic mode. Internally I felt nervous, on edge. My brain wouldn't stop thinking negative thoughts.

The image of my fiancée Liz popped into my mind. I knew she would be at work but I needed to call her. Something was wrong; I could sense it. I rushed as fast as I could to the antique school desk where our old-style phone sat. It was one of those phones where you put your finger into each number on the receiver and dialled it, then waited as the receiver clicked back into position. Terror built up inside me as I waited for the number to engage.

"Be there...please be there," I muttered to myself.

The phone seemed to ring for ages and ages. In truth, it was probably about 15 seconds. But that was 15 long seconds of silence bashing at the inside of my brain, like someone kicking a football into my face. My heart was beating so hard it seemed to pound against the walls of my chest. I sat there, short of breath, with wild thoughts spinning around my head, my imagination going completely out of control.

'What if she's dead?'

'What if she's been kidnapped?'

'What if she's been involved in a car crash?'

Looking back now it was such a bizarre way to act. I didn't know why then, all of a sudden, I thought something bad had happened to my fiancée of six months. I gripped the receiver tightly in my sweaty palm.

Someone from the reception at her office answered.

"Extension 3106 please," I yelled quickly, down the phone.

There was another long wait as I was connected. More unpleasant scenarios played out in my mind.

"Hello. Liz speaking," she said.

On hearing her voice, the relief I felt was indescribable. An invisible weight lifted off my shoulders. However, the joy was short-lived. I couldn't actually speak to her. Instead, I broke down into uncontrollable tears. Over the years since that day, I've found out when someone suffering from depression starts crying it's like having the hiccups. There's nothing really you can do to stop it. Someone leaping out of the bushes isn't going to scare you into stopping, someone sneaking up behind you and bursting a brown paper bag behind your back isn't going to cause you to suddenly stop either. Like the hiccups you've just got to let it take its course.

"Hello?" she repeated several times.

I sat on the chair by the desk, shaking. I felt as if I was closing in on myself. My self-esteem was gently ebbing away, like the air from a slow puncture, until I was utterly deflated.

I finally muttered some words. "Hi Liz it's me."

"Phil...Phil what's wrong?"

Tears streamed down my face. "Nothing...I just wanted to hear your voice." I put the phone down and cried and cried until there were no more tears left.

That was the day depression first came knocking at my door. It's been a regular visitor ever since.

2

My Family and Other 'A' Levels

'Phil Steele embodies the heart and soul of Welsh rugby at every level, and that is not easy. He takes care of the grass roots whilst also commanding an authoritative view on the top echelon of the game. You'd be hard-pressed to find anyone in Wales who has the passion, care and commitment for Welsh rugby as Phil showcases in every facet of his life, and not just in the media. He is a natural communicator, and manages to touch the hearts and minds of every person involved in the game in Wales. His humour is infectious, and it is borne out of the very soul of Welshness, found in rugby communities, in the villages and even in the big cities. Phil's ability to capture the serious subject of rugby and wrap it around a healthy dose of humour is the very essence of life in Wales.'

Alan Wilkins
Broadcaster

I'm not saying for one minute that the Catholic Church purposely led me, barefooted, down the road towards a town called depression. However, somewhere along the line, I believe it did subconsciously steer me along that path. For starters, it can't be healthy having all that guilt, damnation and the 'burning in the fires of hell' thrust upon someone at such a young age. It seemed like the only school trips we went on were guilt trips! Therefore I think it did have some kind of bearing on what happened to me later in my life.

My mother was a staunch Catholic. If you cut her in half, the letters 'R.C.' would have been running right through her, like some kind of religious stick-of-rock. She held such strong Catholic beliefs that I'm really not sure how her and my dad, a protestant, actually got together in the first place. In the early part of the 20th century, mixed religious marriages were quite rare in Wales. In fact they were frowned upon, by both sides. Even during their wedding service at St. David's Catholic Church in Cardiff, on 30th September 1944, they weren't allowed to have the banns read out, weren't allowed to have a nuptial mass, or even have the organ played. I guess, as the song goes, love moves in mysterious ways.

My mother Nancy came into this world in central Cardiff at the start of May 1922. My father Jack was born 27 days later in the Adamsdown area of the city.

My dad contracted polio at a young age. No one was sure how he caught it, but unfortunately for him, and many others at that time, it was just before the vaccinations were introduced. This left him with his leg in irons for most of his boyhood, meaning that he had no muscle in his left leg and the disease left him with a limp for the rest of his life. Did this affect him? Well, he was never able to play sports like most kids and struggled to kick a ball, so I assume it did but he never really talked about it. He was one of those men who just got on with whatever life had to throw at him.

Every Sunday when I was growing up, I would always go with Dad when he drove my nan back home to her house in Roath. On the return journey he would stop off at Roath 'Rec', where I would have a kick about for half an hour but Dad always stayed in the car. Once I asked him to stand at the end of the field so I could kick the ball to him. He tried to kick it back, but struggled, limping about. I tried my hardest to make sure the ball landed right by him, which was a great way to improve my soccer skills but I feel terrible for saying that I felt sorry for him as I watched him hobble about. I can only begin to imagine just how he must have felt. It must have been awful for him not to be able to kick a ball back to his 13-year-old son. Dads are supposed to be superheroes and invincible in the eyes of their children.

My parents met while they were both working on the railways during the war – because of my dad's disability he couldn't serve in the military. My mum was a ticket collector; a protected occupation during those dark times.

I never met my grandparents on my mother's side. My mother's mother died of pneumonia in her early 40s, whilst my mother's father served in the Great War and was awarded the Mons Star medal. He was gassed in action during his military service and, although he survived, he struggled with his health from then on, finding it hard to breathe properly and always having a bad chest. He died the night after my mother and father got married in 1944. It probably wasn't the best of honeymoons, that's for sure.

What's more, my mother, who was still a relatively young woman at the tender age of 23, became the legal guardian of her sister, my Auntie Eileen, who lived with my parents until she got married in 1957. Over those thirteen years, my Auntie Eileen was effectively brought up as another sister, alongside my elder sister Trisha.

My parents first lived in a small house in Treharris Street, Roath, which they shared with my nan, my father's mother. It was your typical, two up, two down Cardiff terraced house, where they endured the hardship of the war like most people across the city.

My eldest sister, Trisha, was born in July 1945, about a year after my parents were married and in May 1950 they all moved into a house on the brand new council estate of Caerau, in the Ely district on the western side of the city. At the time it must have seemed like Shangri-La to them and they lived in the same house, 81 Heol Eglwys, until they died in the 1980's. Even then, their attachment to that house was such that their bodies reposed in the house rather than in a funeral home prior to their burials.

My brother, John, came along in 1957 and I followed suit not long after, in 1961 when my parents were both 39. I was always conscious, as I grew up, that my parents were 'old'. That's unfair on them but all my friend's mams and dads just seemed, looked and were, much younger. At that time they were considered quite old to have kids. Today it's not a big deal, but then it must have been, especially when my younger sister, Ann, came along four years later, when my mother was touching 43 years of age. Like me, Ann was born in our house not in the hospital and I remember the night well. Mrs Bowen, our next door neighbour, delivered her in my parent's bedroom. All the running about and the screaming and panic...and that was just me and my brother! My dad was still in work and missed the whole thing.

I was always conscious when growing up that my parents were old. That's unfair on them but all my friends' mams and dads just seemed, looked and were, much younger.

If my mother was the fount of all religious knowledge, my father was definitely the Encyclopaedia Britannica of the railway network. He knew every train and every track in the country. He was your typical, old fashioned, railway man, always smartly dressed in his railway uniform and always on time for whatever he did, but he always seemed to be at work. I can still picture him now, either coming home from, or going to, work on his small motorbike. I felt great comfort on hearing the sound of the engine pulling up outside our house. Knowing he was home safe, meant I could sleep easy.

I never heard him swear, not once. Not even a 'bloody hell'. For everything he had to put up with, he must have been some kind of a saint.

He worked for the same company for all of his life, starting as a messenger boy and working his way up to becoming a guard and eventually a supervisor. He loved his job with a passion. If someone mentioned trains or the rail system you could see a light shining bright in his eyes. His knowledge of the railways was phenomenal. If he could have gone on the TV programme *Mastermind* to answer questions on his chosen subject of the railway network, I would have bet my mortgage on him winning it hands down. I recall someone at Cardiff General (now Cardiff Central) station once asking him how to get to somewhere like King's Lynn. Without a second thought, he replied, "You take the 10.15 to Birmingham, change at ... .'

One of his party pieces was to recite every station, and I mean even the tiny 'halts', to every destination for trains departing from Cardiff General. It rubbed off on us kids because, even today, I'm able to put my invisible anorak on and list all the stations from Cardiff to Portsmouth Harbour and Cardiff to Newcastle, which I learned from mimicking my dad! My brother and I became train spotters more by default than desire.

Like a lot of families in Ely at that time, we were quite poor. Even though my eldest sister had left home, they still had three children to bring up. My mother wasn't working at the time, so we survived on my father's railwayman's wages. Mum would always be patching up our jeans or getting our shoes resoled. We never ate out. On our trips it was always sandwiches and flasks of tea. On saying that, we never went short of anything either. If I needed new football boots or if I wanted to go, with my brother, to see Cardiff City play, there was always money there for us. Looking back now they must have sacrificed a lot, like most parents in Ely do for their kids.

All our holidays had a link to the railways in some way, shape or form. Because of cheap rail fares for employees, we always found ourselves holidaying close to train routes. Jersey and Guernsey were popular destinations – the train to Weymouth then the ferry across to the Channel Islands. I knew more about Jersey and Guernsey than I did about parts of Cardiff, but it was great for us kids. We would even go on long day trips, such as travelling to Boulogne in France, and not get off the boat! My parents would stock up on the 'duty free' and we'd all head home again. Once we even ventured all the way to Carlisle, before heading back to Cardiff only 20 minutes after arriving! A torture more than a holiday for some, but we enjoyed it.

My parents were incredibly proud of their house, which they'd bought from the council in 1969. My father's first DIY job on his 'own' home was to scale a ladder, roller in hand, to paint it a different colour to the other houses on the estate. That must have been like a badge of honour for them.

What I remember about our house was it always seemed to be full to the brim with people, who'd be laughing, drinking tea – or often something a little stronger. I don't know if it was a Catholic thing or just a Welsh thing but I seemed to have loads of aunties and uncles – there appeared to be hundreds of them. They would all pop by after church or be there when I got home from school. Auntie Julie, Auntie Winnie, Auntie Kath, Uncle Jake and Uncle Billy Guilfolyle. The list went on and on. If one of the priests from our church, St. Francis, called by, my mum would get out the best china tea-set. A visit from the priest was like a visit from the Queen.

My parents, both big Cardiff City fans, loved sport. My mother was one of those people who couldn't control her emotions. When watching Wales play rugby, she would be jumping up and down, screaming at the TV. She would cheer, laugh, and cry in equal measures – a right mixed bag of emotions. On match day we'd turn the settee around to face the TV, clamber on it and pretend it was the North Stand at Cardiff Arms Park. We still only had a black and white TV and most of the time the picture was so bad we couldn't see anything, or it just packed in altogether. My dad would be forever hitting it or moving it to get a better signal. It was always when something I really wanted to watch was on. The next morning in school, all the kids would be talking about a programme they'd watched the night before and I'd have to pretend I'd seen it.

Mrs Thomas, next door, had a colour TV. A real one and the first one on the street. On match days we would often be waiting, peeking out of the curtains and holding our breath for her to knock our door and ask if we would like to come over to her house to watch the game.

A man holding an elephant gun couldn't have stopped us. I was like Colin Jackson vaulting over our furniture in our front room to get out of the door and into her house.

The most memorable match I saw on her TV, the one which still sticks in my mind, was when Gareth Edwards scored his famous try against Scotland at the Arms Park in 1972. Seeing him walk back to the half way line, his chest pumped out with pride and his face covered in the red mud from the old greyhound track is an image I'll go to my grave with. Mrs Thomas' colour television was a gift from the gods.

The Steele family were all rugby nuts but, probably more surprisingly, my mother also loved boxing. Quite a contradiction I suppose given her strong religious beliefs. The rosary and the boxing glove isn't an image which automatically springs to mind, though she was always keen to remind us that the great

Cardiff boxer 'Peerless' Jim Driscoll was a Catholic and donated much of his prize money to Nazareth House – a Catholic nursing home in the city. But her love for the sport changed on the tragic day Johnny Owen, the boxer from Merthyr, died in America after getting knocked out by the Mexican fighter, Lupe Pintor. I don't think she ever watched a boxing match after that.

Just as much as watching games live, I also loved to listen to my dad telling us stories about all the sporting stars of yesteryear. Players such as footballers John Charles, Trevor Ford, Ivor Allchurch and Alf Sherwood, and rugby players Haydn Tanner, Cliff Morgan, Bleddyn Williams and Dr Jack Mathews. I knew all about the rugby, football and cricket greats even though I'd never seen them. His knowledge and storytelling was second to none. I never got tired of hearing tales about Bleddyn's brilliant sidestepping. "He could sidestep the grass," my father would say. Or Dr Jack, who would "knock players out on the field with a vicious tackle on a Saturday and then be stitching them up in his doctor's surgery on the Monday."

My dad took me and my brother to watch Cardiff City and Cardiff RFC a few times. Going to those matches left a big impression on me. I loved everything about the day. I even became a ball boy at Cardiff RFC for 3 seasons from the age of 12.

If my father knew that many years later, through my work as a broadcaster and after-dinner speaker, I would be on first name terms with Bleddyn and Jack he would have been be so proud. Similarly, I have to pinch myself these days when I think that I am on similar familiar terms with many of my great heroes. To be called by my first name by the likes of Gareth Edwards, Barry John and Gerald Davies is still a huge thrill.

These legendary sporting figures made a great impact on me as I grew up, with my memory replaying their thrilling exploits again and again. I'm not sure that kids have that as much today. Maybe it's the proliferation of sport on TV but they don't seem to have the same sense of the history of the game and where it came from. Even today I can name nearly every team of the 70s and 80s. Although, I think I would struggle to do that for the 90s to the present day!

My abiding memory of growing up was of always being outdoors; either playing some game, or climbing trees, or playing down by the river. I was never at home except for arriving back for tea. It was just great being out all the time, enjoying myself and not worrying about anything. It wasn't like today. There didn't seem to be the same sorts of fears and dangers back then. Or it didn't feel like it anyway. But I also think summers were warmer and winters were colder back in those good old days, so who knows.

If I close my eyes and think back, I always had a ball with me, wherever I went. I'd spend hours in the street, kicking it back and forth. Our house was located at the end of the terrace, with a big privet hedge which doubled up as the posts of the Arms Park or the goals at Ninian Park or Wembley. Often the ball would hit someone's car or sail over into a neighbour's garden. If the ball went in to Mr Green's garden, we knew we were in trouble. He was the killjoy, the Antichrist of kid's ball games. He'd always rush out, in his vest like he'd just shaved, and give us a right old rollicking.

"Can't you take the bloody ball down the bloody fields and get it away from my car," he'd bellow.

Ironically, later when I got to play for Newport Rugby Club, he would always stop me to say well done.

'Yeah, no thanks to you mate,' I thought.

When I got a little older I graduated to playing on the tump of grass known as 'the green' a few streets over, with the bigger boys. To us kids, however, it was much more than just a big tump of grass. It was the big tump of grass which held every FA Cup and World Cup Final you could ever imagine (jumpers for goal posts and all that). It was serious stuff – the big time! We even put our proper kits and boots on and would play on it for hours and hours. I learnt to kick a rugby ball on that special piece of grass. Hours were spent booting it from one end to the other and hopefully not hitting any passing cars, buses or the odd pedestrian.

In the summer, the football posts – aka jumpers – were stored away and about 30 of us would turn 'the green' into Lords Cricket Ground, with me in the guise of Glamorgan's Alan Jones or Majid Khan. On other occasions the pavement around the street would turn into the 100 metre track at the 1972 Munich Olympics where I'd suddenly transform into the brilliant 100 metre Russian sprinter, Valeriy Borzov. Nothing could stop me.

I was always playing, competing and at times holding my own against the older kids which gave me a lot of confidence. It also got me into trouble on many occasions. I'm not saying we were troublemakers, far from it, but we often played the odd game of 'Rat-a-tat Ginger' where we would knock on someone's door and run away. I think it's called 'Rat-a-tat Parcel Force Delivery' nowadays!

I always tagged along with my older brother, John, and his mates. As well as playing football together, when John was older he used to take me to watch Cardiff City. Our mother would give us two shillings for the bus to Ninian Park and the match ticket. Being crafty we would walk to Leckwith to save our money for pie and chips on the walk home. John also had a fantastic knowledge of sport but it was music which was his first love. If you played a record he could name the artist, what year it was a hit and where it reached in the charts before the chorus started.

I never spent much time with my eldest sibling, Trisha, as she left to get married when I was aged about ten. She did well for herself and went on to become a teacher, moving to live in Culverhouse Cross at the top of Ely – the posh part as we called it! There was a 20 year gap between her and my youngest sister and Trisha actually taught Ann in St. Francis Infants School. One day she covered my class because my teacher was ill and I accidently called her Trish in front of everyone. I remember the stare she shot at me. You could hear a pin drop.

Of all my siblings, it was Ann, my youngest sister, I was closest to in both age and personality. She was a very talented girl and won several writing competitions. We'd spend hours together just talking and laughing and having fun.

As I mentioned, my mother was extremely religious. If awards had been handed out for being spiritual she would have easily won an Oscar (or a Papal BAFTA) for the most religious person in the city. She was also very caring and generous. Even though we never had much she would go out of her way to help people worse off than us and she insisted on upholding traditional social and moral values. But, on the odd occasion she let fly, she had a temper to match a six foot docker on strike. 'The Wrath of Nance', we called it.

When I was about 10, I stayed out with my mates and came home later than I should have. My parents didn't know where I was. They were worried sick. When I eventually ventured back, my mother didn't mess about. Out came the dreaded, small, cricket bat-shaped piece of plywood that hung on the kitchen wall near the cooker and I had six of the best. I remember my grandmother pleading with my mother to stop, but she didn't listen. She was like Gary Sobers hitting his famous six sixes out of the ground at Swansea on my behind. I couldn't sit down for days. I never stayed out late again!

She also put great store on education. She was so proud if we did well at our studies. I think because my mother left school when she was 14 to look after her father – who had health problems after the war – as well as her younger sister and brother, she thought she had missed out on such an important part of her development in life. She didn't sit the 11-Plus or any other exams and she didn't want the same thing to happen to us. If I brought a school report home and one of the teachers had said, something like, 'Phil is a pleasure to teach.' I could see the smile fixed on her face for the rest of the day.

My parents also impressed on us all the importance of manners. I can remember my mother repeating to us many times, "It's, 'please may I have'," or "It's not 'what?', It's 'pardon'."

My Uncle Michael, a real uncle this time, my mother's older brother, owned a hardware store in Stoke-on-Trent . His wife ran a ladies clothes shop as well. To my mother they were the top end of posh. We usually ventured up to see them once or twice a year, using one of the six free tickets my father was given annually as a perk of his job with the railway.

For weeks before we visited, my mother would make us all practise our table manners and our handshakes. On one occasion she even threw a spot of role-playing into the mix. She sat in our kitchen pretending to be our Uncle Michael and we stood out in the hallway. On the count of four, I opened the door and walked in.

"Hello," I said, with a huge smile.

My mother had a fit. "No! It's not 'hello'. It's, 'How do you do'."

She made us practice it again and again until everything was perfect. Even today when people shake my hand I can see them wincing in pain as I unintentionally squeeze their hand to a pulp.

There was also a big insistence on good manners, punctuality and even writing letters. She would make us write it out on scrap paper first, and then she would check it for spelling and punctuation before she would allow us to write it on the proper paper. It was only after these checks and double checks had been made that the Basildon Bond paper (the best paper around at that time) would be brought out of the desk and handed to us as if it was a plate of her best china. Even when addressing the envelope, if we wrote the address too high she would make us do it again. She didn't want the postmark to block out the writing.

I know I'm making her out to be a nit-picker, but she meant well; there's nothing wrong with good manners, being on time and doing things right. A bit more of these three things would make the world a better place.

Telling the truth was probably on top of her 'Must Do' list. I wouldn't dare lie to her. Even to this day I'm a hopeless liar and, from my one and only past experience, an even worse thief. There was a little sweet shop on the road near our school in Ely, owned by Harry Jennings. It was one of those timeworn, dusty old shops, crammed full of a million and one items, with boiled sweets of all colours and sizes packed in to jars taking up every inch of space. I think the owner must have suffered from Parkinson's disease or a similar condition as, in addition to being old and slow, he shook quite a lot if my memory serves me correctly. When he used to go out the back to get something, all the kids would pinch things off the counter. I never did. I was always too scared. Then one day, when I was around nine or ten, temptation popped up in the form of a little, mischievous, red devil on my shoulder egging me on. When the shopkeeper turned around to get something, I reached across and slipped a white chocolate mouse into the pocket of my duffle coat. I'm not sure if he could see by my face that I'd nicked something or he'd suddenly grown another set of eyes in the back of his head but he walked straight up to me, put his hand straight in my pocket and pulled out the stolen chocolate. He went spare, calling me every name under, and over, and on, the sun. In tears, I rushed out, my head hung in shame. Then the guilt kicked in. I wasn't right for days. I lay in bed imagining the worst. I pictured Mr Jennings coming around to tell my parents about the 'great white chocolate mouse robbery of 1971'. I suspect my mother would have died of shame right there in the hallway, or more likely reached for the cricket bat!

I worried myself sick. What if the teachers in school found out, or my friends, or the priest, the nuns, even the Pope himself? I pictured the headlines in the the *South Wales Echo*; 'Steele steals white mouse – Read the inside story of a poor defenceless chocolate mouse's terrifying ordeal in a stranger's pocket!'

On a serious note, I really couldn't sleep or eat as those thoughts kept playing out in my head. I couldn't shake off the worry of the consequences and I never went in that shop ever again. If I ever had to walk past it, it was always with my head down and eyes fixed to the pavement.

Even from an early age, I must have always been overly sensitive with a strong sense of worry rooted deep inside me. Sometimes even the smallest thing would cause me to be riddled with guilt and anxiety. My 'worry meter' must have been set to 'super sensitive' and once it was triggered, it would constantly nag away at me.

The feeling came over me in waves. Around that time, I went through a strange phase when washing my face and brushing my teeth before going to bed. I would do the oddest thing. In the bathroom, I wouldn't or couldn't leave unless I had folded all the towels and the flannels properly and put them all in order. Then I made sure the soap was clean. I know that sounds silly, but I would wash the soap and the soap dish until there were no marks or mess on it. I'd convinced myself that if I didn't do this something terrible would happen to me, I was going to die in my sleep or something bad was going to happen to my mum and dad. Every time they went out I would worry they wouldn't come back. I would try and force myself to go to sleep early because I didn't want to panic if they were a few minutes late coming home. It didn't work. More often than not I would lie there, wide awake, late into the night until they returned.

If I knew in advance that they would be out on a certain night, I could actually feel the anxiety starting to build a few days before. A gradual feeling of doom and foreboding – like knowing you had a visit to the dentist coming up – but ten times worse.

I'd always been quite big for my age but even my size didn't stop the worrying about the most basic of things, even rugby. It was at at St. Francis primary school in Ely that I played my first proper organised game of rugby. I idolised Mr Pearce, our sports teacher. Even at that young age he taught me the basics of rugby and how to play it in the right spirit. Once, Mr Pearce lambasted me and another boy, David Sexton, in front of all the other boys for not putting enough effort it.

David laughed the rollicking off. He was that type of boy but I couldn't. It stuck with me – continually niggling away. The teacher's words lodged in my throat then stuck in the pit of my stomach. I have always been the type of person that needed reassurance. I needed someone to tell me how good I was. If someone told me I was a good player, I would be good but if someone didn't give me the confidence, I'd go to pieces. Stupid things would play on my mind. Stupid things would burden me and weigh me down as if someone had filled my boots with lead.

Later in life when I played for Newport, our captain, the great Mike 'Spikey' Watkins, could sense this about me almost straight away. In the changing rooms before going out to play, he used to look me in the eye. "Steeley," he'd say with pride, "you are the best full-back in Wales. You are so good the selectors are here just to see you. Show them how good you are."

He made me feel two hundred feet tall. I'd run through a brick wall to get out on that field for 'Spikey'.

In retrospect, even at school I must have suffered from anxiety. Some days, like the incident with the white mouse or getting told off by the teacher, I would be terrified. I would sit in my bedroom and imagine the world was against me. Yet there was another part of me which was completely the opposite. In form two – now called year eight – at the Archbishop Mostyn High School, which I attended after leaving St. Francis, I took part in the school production of Oliver. I played the knife-grinder in the chorus. It was only a small part but I loved it. The feeling I got from standing on the stage – being out in front of the audience – was divine. I loved the applause, the attention, I loved it all. I think I must have always been an entertainer. I've always felt happy when making people laugh. Even at primary school there was always a performer inside me, bursting to get out.

One day during an RE lesson, taught by a kindly but rather stern-faced Nun named Sister Michael, we were reading a text book which mentioned the Val Doonican song, *Walk Tall*. I knew the song, as my elder sister Tricia had a Val Doonican LP.

"Anyone know the song?" asked Sister Michael.

My hand shot up.

"Would you like to sing it?" she added, expecting me to be mortified at having to sing a song in front of my classmates.

Instead of declining, I marched to the front of the class and began belting it out, word for word. For those three minutes, all my fears and anxieties melted away. I was the star, not the boy riddled with apprehension. It wasn't a big deal for me. I didn't even blush. The irony of having the confidence to get up and sing that particular song has often struck me, because for much of my life, as you will find out, I haven't been able to walk tall, at all!

Thinking back now, the whole coldness and power of the church and religion scared me and confused me. Going to confession, I think, scarred many people for life. I hated going there. Walking into that small, confined box was like walking to the electric chair. Not that I had much to confess when I was nine years of age. I used to sit there, desperately trying to think of what terrible sins I had committed that past week. Other than stealing the white mouse, I wasn't that bad really.

I used to make most of it up. I remember we had a book to help us called *The Simple Prayer Book* – you could buy it for a shilling. I made my First Confession at the age of seven. I can still remember the actual date, that's how bad it was! My big day was 21 May 1968 – a few days before my First Communion. It was like studying for an 'A' level in 'Guilt'. I even remember the Priest, he was Canon Cahill.

"Bless me Father for I have sinned, this is my first confession." Then I'd sit there thinking of my sins. Maybe I should have written it all down but I don't think you were allowed to do that, or maybe I didn't want my mother to see it.

He asked me what I'd done wrong so I looked at the prayer book and reeled off a few of the things on the list without understanding what I was admitting to. "Well father...I've coveted my neighbour's ox. No, I haven't killed anyone but I've definitely committed adultery...I think about six times." I thought adultery meant behaving like a grown up and I couldn't understand why it was classed as a sin given that our teachers were always telling us we should behave more maturely and sensibly! I never mentioned stealing the white mouse!

Whilst preparing for First Confession we learned about venial and mortal sins. If you carried out a mortal sin that was the end of you. Missing Mass on a Sunday was, for example, considered a mortal sin. That fear stayed with me well into adulthood. As a rugby player I have been on tours in many different countries and not gone to bed until very late on a Saturday night but have somehow still got up and found a church so I could go to Mass on the Sunday.

I went to confession virtually every week when I was in junior school. What a great feeling when you came out of confession on that Saturday morning. 'YESSSS…I'm clean…I'm off now to commit adultery with my neighbour's ox.'

Of course, with my mother the way she was, we always went to Mass on Sundays. All of us kitted-out in Sunday best, with me in starched collars and washed behind the ears.

My mother always wanted me to be an altar boy. To be honest I remember being quite thrilled when I got accepted to join the altar boys when I was about eight or nine.

Mr Brookes, a great chap, was the man in charge. He seemed to know absolutely everything about who should do what, when and how during Mass or other services such as Benediction. He was organised and inspirational, the Carwyn James of the altar boys! The way he was able to choreograph and manoeuvre twelve altar boys and a priest seamlessly into a procession and then into position was as impressive as a move by the All Blacks! I can almost hear the dulcet tones of Jonathan Davies analysing some of Mr Brookes' handiwork: "Look, the two candle carriers go to the left, the server carrying the cross moves to the right, the kid with incense acts as a dummy runner so there's numbers on the left and BANG, there he is – the Priest goes straight through the middle up to the altar to start the Mass. That's great play and the congregation are on their feet!"

On Thursday evening, altar boy practise took place. It was like playing in a rugby trial game. There would have been about 20 boys there, all wanting to outdo each other. On the Friday, the list would go up in the vestry detailing which boys were serving which Mass on the Sunday. We'd would all rush and barge to the front to see if we had been selected to serve or 'picked to play' in the big one – the 11am High Mass! If your name was there it was as if you had been selected to play for the Lions against the All Blacks. It was better still if you got to carry the candle – you were vice-captain – and if, on the off chance, you got to actually walk at the front with the incense, that was it, you had made it – the Willie John McBride of the altar boys.

In those days, the 11am Mass was a glamorous gig to get for any up-and-coming altar boy. It was usually attended by a couple of hundred people – men, women and children – all crammed into the church, as well as the choir, organist and most of the teachers from school. If Sky TV had been around in those days, they would have been there covering it live!

If I found myself as replacement, or first sub, for the Sunday Mass, that Saturday night I would get down on my knees and pray to God. *'Dear God...Please can you make Jonny Jones ill tomorrow. Nothing too serious, maybe pull a hamstring while stretching in the vestry. Ps but can you ensure Jonny is better by Wednesday because we have a big rugby match against St Josephs.'*

I rarely got the honour. Nine times out of ten I got selected to be involved in the 8 o'clock Mass but I didn't mind that. No one else wanted to do it and what's more, I had the rest of the day free to do what I wanted to do. There would also only be about 40 people in the congregation unlike the hundreds who would turn up for the Test Match that was the 11 o'clock Mass.

My father, not being Catholic, never went to church. For

his sins, he would stay home and make us all a great cooked breakfast on our return.

After primary school, I progressed to Archbishop Mostyn High School in Ely, Cardiff.

Whilst the Catholic Church was an important part of my upbringing and still retains a strong influence on my life, I lived and breathed rugby and, after moving up to secondary school, this devotion to the oval-ball game flourished – with the help of some fantastic PE teachers. John Evans played for Cardiff and later for Penarth. I remember going to watch the Snelling Sevens at the Arms Park and Mr Evans was playing. His standing instantly went up in my eyes. This was my own teacher playing at the Arms Park. Another teacher was Beverley Davies. He had played for Cardiff against South Africa and also ran out for Llanelli against the mighty All Blacks in 1963. He was a legend. My father once found a discarded rugby book, *The Fifth All Blacks*, on the train and brought it home for me and my brother. Written by the legendary Welsh rugby journalist J.G.B. Thomas, the book was packed full of facts and figures of the All Blacks tour of the British Isles in 1963 and how Newport had beaten them, the only side to do so on that tour. Mr Davies' name was in there. I was so proud. The both of them were your typical Welsh rugby-mad sports teachers. They oozed life and of course rugby. They were very knowledgeable men and I loved the way they spoke in their strong west Wales accents.

I also had the pleasure of being taught by Alan Mould. He was more of an all-round sportsman and played football, rugby and cricket for local clubs. He encouraged us to play different sports, such as basketball, which I believe are vital in the development, not only of specific ball skills but also as they engender a respect of all sports and those who play them.

When I was about 16 I joined the cricket club at Wenvoe, a small village on the way to Barry, about three miles from Ely. I used to open the batting with a lovely man and very talented cricketer named Mike Howells. The trouble was, Mike was also the deputy headmaster of Mostyn School. When I'd play a shot and say, "Sir...there's a run there", or, "Good shot Sir!" the other team used to snigger. To compound a strange situation, if Mike got out, the next batsman was Alan Mould – my PE teacher! There were more "Yes Sirs!" and "No Sirs!" than the Army on parade. The opposition must have thought I was the politest cricketer in the whole of Wales

Of course, school wasn't just about rugby and cricket and, without wanting to come across as big-headed, I sailed through my 'O' levels. I even achieved a grade A in Human Biology in my fourth year, twelve months before I was supposed to take the exam – despite the section on contraception having been physically removed from the chapter on reproduction in our text books. Contraception was obviously considered to be a mortal sin even though it didn't even warrant a passing mention in *The Simple Prayer Book*.

A year on, after my Human Biology triumph, I got As and Bs in all my other subjects. I liked school and I enjoyed all the subjects, except for Art. I hated the subject with such a passion, that I gave it up in form three and took Spanish instead – and I didn't really like Spanish either!

Why would I give up Art? Subconsciously I knew that if I drew something and it was terrible then it was there for everyone to see, for everyone to ridicule. I imagined the Art teacher pinning my work onto the classroom wall, or worse still the staff room wall, so everyone could laugh at it. I never gave it a chance. Those few hours every week attempting to be 'arty' were pure torture. I'd rather have had pins stuck in my eyes. In form four I dropped music as well, which in hindsight was a mistake. I love music now, either listening to it, or playing it myself.

I wonder what my music teacher would have said if he'd known that years later, during the Rugby World Cup in 1999, I'd be appearing on BBC Radio Wales as a lyricist singing four self-composed topical songs a week, live, for six weeks.

Having done so well in my 'O' levels I decided to go into the sixth form to take 'A' levels. Initially I made a mistake by taking English but after a few weeks I switched to Geology – I found shales and schists easier than Shakespeare. I still find it weird that people write books trying to explain what Dylan Thomas or Chaucer meant when they wrote a poem or story, but how do they know? Then someone else would write another book critiquing the book which critiqued the poem. It all seemed so bizarre. Despite this I do have a love for language and I love to embrace it and experiment with it during my commentaries and match reports.

Whilst doing my English 'O' level I had three books to cover; William Golding's *Lord of the Flies*, *Our Town* the play by Thornton Wilder and Shakespeare's *Julius Caesar*. To this day I still haven't read any of them fully, yet I passed my English Literature 'O' Level exam with a grade B. Does that mean I knew literature or was I just good at regurgitating quotations?

Along with Geology I studied Geography and Biology at 'A' level to go along with my by now extremely well developed 'A' level in 'Guilt'!

I particularly enjoyed Geography and ended up achieving a grade A, which delighted my teacher Mr Dewi Evans, as A grades were much rarer then than they are today.

I also enjoyed Biology – except for when it came to practical examinations. Part of the exam was to dissect a rat. It wasn't that I was squeamish and found it gory or anything. It was just that I wasn't good with my hands. Even today DIY and I are uneasy bedfellows. I would rather run 25 miles in the rain than try and put a picture up in the front room.

I knew that in the exam we would be asked to do one of three dissections; cut through the urinary genital system – which is slicing through the testicles and all that bollocks (pun intended) – the digestive system or the neck and thorax. I didn't mind the first two but the one I didn't want during the exam was to perform on the neck and the thorax in which you had to clearly show the heart, lungs and trachea together with various blood vessels, including the all-important aorta. I was quite big guy with big fingers and this was far too precise for me. If they had asked me to cut the neck and thorax of a buffalo with a hacksaw, a lump hammer and pliers that wouldn't have been a problem. I could have done it with one hand behind my back and probably blindfolded. Unfortunately, as it was a rat, it felt to me like trying to write your name and address on the back of a postage stamp with a paint brush.

I was so worried, about the neck and thorax dissection I used to buy dead rats from the school for 60p a pop to practice on at home, feeling like Ely's very own Dr Frankenstein or perhaps Doctor Cutuparat.

I'd park myself at an old table in the garage and stay in there for hours cutting up poor rodents and trying to get it right, though I never did. That was the time I needed someone like a 'Spikey' Watkins to tell me I was the best rat cutter-upper in the world and the rat cutter-upper selectors were in the crowd (or sitting on the shelf where my dad kept the old cans of paint) and show them how good I was. But he wasn't there.

The fact that I couldn't do the neck and thorax operation played on my mind. I prayed the night before the exam it would be one of the other two. Alas, God either wasn't listening or he wanted to have some fun at my expense that day because when I turned the paper over, there it was. The question I had been dreading.

- *Make a dissection of the neck and thorax of rattus norvegicus* (the biological name for the rat).
- *Show the following organs and structures: The heart, lungs, trachea, aorta, superior and inferior vena cavae, pulmonary artery and vein.*
- *Draw a labelled diagram of your dissection.*

I began to sweat like a snowman in a sauna as I cut into the rat's chest with a scalpel. What didn't help was the two girls doing the exam at the same time looked like they were born to perform the operation. They had delicate little fingers seemingly just made for messing about inside rats. Here was I, cutting and tearing, poking and prodding – the right hand not even knowing what the right hand was doing, never mind what the left hand was doing.

My motto had been, 'if in doubt cut it out', and after 45 minutes of my best handiwork, I straightened up to survey the damage. I could have burst into tears. To be honest it would have looked more professional if I had strapped a small bomb to the rat's chest and just detonated it. It looked like it had been in a car crash. Luckily enough, despite the cack-handed practical, I knew the theory inside out and my diagram of how my dissection should have looked was, well, spot-on. The actual dissection however, looked nothing like it. There was a small bit of the heart left, together with just the left lobe of a lung and the trachea (windpipe). I had even managed to cut through the aorta which now hung limply in two string parts.

Still, 'never say your mother reared a gibber' as we used to say in Ely, and not to be outdone, I took a small dissection pin and joined the two ends together, hiding the pin underneath.

30

The trouble was, the aorta was now as taught as a fiddle string – you could have played a tune on it. *Rat Trap* by The Boomtown Rats sprung to mind.

If the examiner had picked up the rat and turned it over, I'm sure all its insides would have fallen out onto the floor. I bet he was in hysterics behind me as I did the 'Walk of Shame' out of the classroom.

It wasn't surprising that I became a teacher rather than a surgeon!

3

The College of Knowledge

'Phil has an engaging personality & an infectious sense of humour.
As an Ambassador of Wooden Spoon he epitomises what we do
as a children's charity. He enthusiastically supports our fundraising
events including lunches, dinners & social evenings and is a
popular host at our annual quiz.'

Huw Thomas
Chairman, Wooden Spoon Wales

While at Mostyn School I played for the under 15's in the
Cardiff 7's tournament. I must have had a half-decent game,
because when it was over one teacher made a bee-line for me
to see if I would be interested in going to Cardiff to train with
the youth side. Even though I was a big Cardiff fan and had
even been a ball boy at the club when I was younger, I turned
the offer down.

Normally, rugby mad kids would have bitten the guy's arm
off for the opportunity to play for the capital team. Cardiff was
one of the biggest and most famous rugby club sides in the
world in those days. They had more superstars in their ranks
than the city had buses. Only the best of the best got asked to
go there. But there was me, yet again, happy to steer my own

course. Phil Steele, the boy who wasn't content unless he was swimming against the tide, and all that.

Maybe deep down I thought I wasn't ready for the step up and was afraid of getting knocked back. But all I wanted to do was to go and play for Glamorgan Wanderers.

What more can I say? Everyone thought I was mad but I had mates playing for the Wanderers. I felt at ease there. They were my blue, black and white-hooped, comfort blanket.

Although I was still in form five at school, I found myself entering the daunting world of youth rugby. Now that was a tough apprenticeship in anyone's book. As I mentioned, I was quite big for my age, so playing in the school side against teenagers my own age hadn't been a problem, in fact I stood out, but playing against boys who were almost 19 proved to be quite scary. At times it felt more like going to war. I honestly found it a bigger step up for me going from school to youth rugby than going from youth rugby to playing in the senior side years later.

I couldn't believe how big these 'boys' were. They looked old; they looked nasty, and they looked hard. They had beards – real men's beards – not bum-fluff like me and my mates. They drove cars. Some of them were miners, with black eyes, blue scars and menacing stares.

I will never forget my debut against Ynysybwl. They had the biggest pack of forwards I'd ever seen anywhere. In their ranks they had the one and only, Staff Jones, who had just won a Wales youth cap. What a beast of a boy. No, let me rephrase that. What a beast. If my memory serves me right, I'm sure they got him on the field by opening his cage and throwing lumps of raw meat in his path. The game was violent and intimidating. Youth rugby always had that 'One in, all in' type of mentality but this was out and out thuggery of the highest (lowest) order. One of their boys smacked one of our

33

forwards for no reason. As our player lay pole-axed on the ground, stars buzzing around his head, the ref stood there, giving the thug a talking to, someone from the crowd shouted, "Come on Ref, you can't send him off for that...their boy is still alive."

It was one of those games!!

There again, times were a lot different back then. The backbone of youth rugby had violence running through it. It was more or less two gangs of teenagers using rugby as an excuse to have a brawl on a Saturday afternoon, legally: *West Side Story* meets *The Warriors*. To me it mirrored what club rugby, other sports and life in general was like at that time in Wales. It was hard, mean and uncompromising.

I played outside half or centre, which meant I was targeted for some real rough-house stuff. At my nice, friendly Catholic school, you wouldn't dare hit anyone whilst playing; otherwise the nuns would be after you. Seven 'Hail Marys' and a sack-full of 'Our Fathers' if you even thought of belting someone in the name of sport. Yet in youth rugby, it was par for the course, especially when we headed up the valleys. Back then, those valleys sides believed that the best way to beat us city slickers, was to kick the shit out of us from the first whistle to the last. They weren't far wrong mind you. Years later, I noticed, it was the same mentality when any senior side from the capital ventured up the same roads to the valleys. Going to places like Maesteg and Pontypridd could be brutal. Those were games where you stood up and faced the music or got trampled into the ground. The older and slightly wiser I got, the more I accepted it.

Blair Evans coached the youth team at the Wanderers when I was playing there. Later, he went on to become chairman of the club. He was a great coach and a lovely man although he was also a very hard task master. Having said that, he also gave lots of teenagers in the area a sense of purpose and pride. Without him really knowing it, he did a great job for the community by stopping many boys from going down the wrong road. He excelled, more than anyone else I've ever known, in taking kids from poorer parts of the city and giving them a chance and some direction in their lives. Like I said, he proved to be a hard task master. He devised drills in which he used to have us carrying logs. He'd have us carrying them over our heads, doing curls, and running around the field with them. There were times when I felt more like a lumberjack than a young rugby player. I still shudder at the words, "Logs above the head and slowly walk to the 25."

We trained up on the field, under the old fashioned halogen lamp floodlights, though the light emitted from them was more a trickle than a flood! Most nights we could hardly see our hands in front of our faces, let alone catch a ball being thrown to us at speed.

In the second row, we had a big, strong boy who looked the part but couldn't catch a bloody cold never mind the ball at the line-outs. At one training session, in the dark conditions under our floodlights, Blair came up with a master plan to cure the boy of his obvious 'illness'. At the line-out, instead of throwing a ball in, he launched a house brick at the boy instead. It did the trick. The lad caught every brick he threw that night and became a much better player. Blair was either way ahead of his time with his bizarre training techniques or he was a total nut-case but I loved him. He was a fabulous bloke for all the youngsters. He looked after us all and I had great respect for him. In fact, everyone did.

During my second year at the Wanderers, the club combined with Llandaff Rugby Club to go on a tour to Toronto during May 1978. We had to do lots of fundraising to organise but it was all worth it in the end. Since that tour I've been all around the world on various rugby tours or on speaking assignments or just reporting on matches, but that trip, above all others, made the biggest impression on me and Toronto still holds a special place in my heart.

For a young 16-year-old Ely boy, whose only experience of the big wide world was sitting on a train clutching homemade cheese sandwiches while exploring the railway lines of the UK, it was unreal. What could be better in life than to travel on a jumbo jet, without my parents and surrounded by my mates, to go to what felt to me like a new world – kitted-out in brand new blazers, ties and kit bags. Nearly 40 years later, I still have my tie in a cupboard and I'm still good friends with one of the Llandaff Youth players I met on that trip – a great guy called Paul Greenley.

The reception we got, everywhere we went in Canada, was unbelievable. They treated us as if we were a top rugby team from Britain. For those 14 days we became teenage superstars. That's how they treat their sports stars, of any age, in that part of the world. In pairs, we stayed at the houses of the parents of the players, the supporters or the teachers. Even the houses seemed like a million miles away from what most of us lived in back in Wales. Most of these families had three cars on the drive. Three cars! We only had one, and it broke down more often than our TV.

Rugby was a very middle class sport there, as it was in most countries with the exception of Wales and New Zealand. Although rugby is not a major sport in Canada and mainly played by people who don't make the American football or hockey leagues, it was still tough. The games were hard. Not in the sense of us winning the matches. In truth we did that easily, playing six games and winning all six. In spite of this, when it came to tackling, these guys were like human torpedoes flying through the air. They took no prisoners. During one game I took a hit, head-on and I swear my teeth shook for about 15 minutes afterwards.

Throughout the trip I felt as though I was representing my country, which made the whole experience even more special. We played combined teams from different regions, so it was a bit like being the British and Irish Lions but on a much smaller scale. Sometimes we would go to the schools during the day. The girls loved our accents and of course we played on it. By the end of that tour I must have sounded more like Richard Burton reading *Under Milk Wood* than the man himself in his prime.

I remember on one occasion one of my team mates, Eamon Holland – the Gavin Henson of his time – got us into trouble. He was tanned and good looking, plus he had all the talent to match. His family were originally from Cork and nothing proved too hot or too heavy for him.

In Canada, 16-year-olds are allowed to drive cars and Eamon couldn't resist the temptation. Not only did he persuade the family he was staying with that he could drive, he somehow talked them in to letting him borrow their big Chevrolet car. One night, with some of the boys piled in the back, he took the car out for a spin. It wasn't surprising that with him driving as if he was starring in the TV show *The Dukes of Hazard*, he'd spun out of control within ten minutes and ended up facing the wrong way on the carriageway. Unsurprisingly, it didn't take long for the police to arrive, lights flashing and guns drawn. They got Eamon up against the side of the car, and were soon frisking him.

"What's your name sonny?" one of the coppers asked.

"Er...Eamon Holland."

"What's your address?"

"13 Howell Road."

"Jeez...Howell Road...where's that?"

"Down Grand Avenue, then turn second left after the school," came back the innocent reply.

Luckily, he got away with just a caution.

For me, that Canada trip summed up what playing rugby was all about. It was about having great experiences both on and off the field and making friends for life.

I guess it was the innocence of bright-eyed youth. Nothing summed that up more perfectly than how Glen Webbe, the brilliant winger who went on to play for Wales, saw the world back then. I grew up with him in Ely and, like Eamon, he was also a very interesting character. He played for Canton Youth, who were our rivals. He was extremely quick but incredibly laid back off the field. He came out with his own brand of innocence when touring South Africa with Wales Youth in 1980, which was still in the era of *apartheid*. When he got back I asked him how he got on and did he experience any issues due to his colour. In a typical Ely boy's response, he cut through all the *apartheid* nonsense and showed it up for all it was. With a big smile he said, "Stella (my nickname) it was great...they even gave me a bus, hotel and cinema all to myself." That was his way of laughing at what was going on in that country. To me with one sentence he showed more intelligence than all the politicians had ever done. What a man!

In between going to Canada and going off to college I lost virtually all my hair. I went almost completely bald within six months. For any man that's bad enough if they've hit 40, so just imagine how it felt at the age of 17. I'm not sure why this happened to me. I don't really remember it worrying me, although I did take a lot of stick from class mates and friends. Of course I'd rather not have been bald, but I saw it as a development in my personality – another case of me steering my own path through the world. I was 6′ 3″, playing youth rugby as an outside half, the tallest player on the field and

38

almost bald. I must have looked like some kind of freak. It was lucky that I had a good sense of humour!

Because I looked much older, I often got challenged about my age when I turned up to play. It got to the stage where I used to have to take my passport to the ground just to prove my age. Before one match against St. Peter's, I came running out on to the pitch and heard one of their supporters yelling out a snide comment, "Oh they're playing their under 21s today are they? Typical!"

I clocked the guy straight away. After the game I tracked him down in the bar. "Look, 3 June 1961, so I am 18," I said as I pushed my passport towards him.

The embarrassment on his face was priceless. I don't know if it satisfied his curiosity or if he felt sorry for me but he apologised and offered to buy me a pint.

Away from the rugby, I passed my three 'A' levels in the July of 1979 and it was time to think about going to college. Ever since I can remember, I'd wanted to be a PE teacher. It's not that I thought I would be a good one. It was just the idea of being out on the rugby field all day, playing with the ball, keeping fit and of course helping to find the next Gareth Edwards or Barry John.

I had an offer to go to Loughborough University; at that time, the biggest and most prestigious PE college in England. My parents were well chuffed. It was a great honour, for them as much as me, but in my heart-of-hearts there was only one place I wanted to go. A week later I was offered a place at Cyncoed College in my hometown. It had just changed its name from Cardiff College of Education to South Glamorgan Institute and I had no doubt in my mind where I wanted to go. Cardiff College was the place where Gareth Edwards, JJ Williams, Allan Martin, John Bevan, Lynn Davies the long jumper and many more had passed through on the road to becoming PE teachers and sporting stars. After a bit of persuading and explaining, my parents finally accepted my decision.

That first day, while walking down the corridor and staring up in awe at all the athletic achievements listed on the walls, I felt as if I was in sporting heaven. Seeing all the names and records set by the different students simply blew me away: Peter Radford's college record for the 100-yard sprint was, for a time, also the world record; Gareth Edwards held the college high hurdles record; JJ Williams the 400m record; and Allan Martin likewise in the hammer. Instantly I felt the history and achievements of the place oozing out of the bricks and mortar. It was only then that it really hit home that I'd been given this wonderful life-changing opportunity.

'Bloody hell,' I thought, 'I'm standing on the shoulders of giants here.' I felt so inspired; not just from the rugby element but from so many of the other sports as well. I couldn't have imagined selecting a better place in the world for me to be at that time in my life. It was a perfect match as I had the freedom and excitement of college life but with my parents living around the corner.

I still recall being given my green college tracksuit with the three white stripes on the arms and the archer's logo on the left breast. I put it on as soon as I could and I don't think I took it off for the entire four years. I would have worn it to funerals and weddings if I'd had my way! I felt so proud of it and what it meant.

Even in my first week I couldn't get over the number of talented individuals I was rubbing shoulders with. For example, in my year alone, there were at least 12 boys who had played rugby for the Welsh Secondary Schools XV. In the fourth year was David James the world student cross-country champion, whilst Greg Thomas, the cricketer who became an England fast bowler, was in my year – and he wasn't even on the PE course.

40

Just strolling down the corridor I recognised so many faces I'd seen on the back pages of the newspapers or on TV – fantastic talented individuals – and here was I, in the same college as them. To be honest I was the only one I'd never heard of!!

In that first week of college, we were all put into mixed ability classes for most subjects. The one thing I was dreading was the swimming trials. To say I'm not the best swimmer in the world is an understatement. The trial took place in the college pool. The water was freezing, and cold enough to induce hypothermia in a polar bear whilst simultaneously curing every strain of Athlete's Foot known to mankind. We were tested and graded on ability. Without too much surprise I got banded in Group Four, affectionately known as 'F Troop'

"Like an octopus caught in a fishing net," was how one of the lecturers had described me.

One advantage of the college being relatively small and on its own self-sustained campus was that everyone really got to know each other well. Better still, for me, the whole college seemed to be dominated by the PE boys. If you were a PE student in the fourth year, and happened to be in the rugby side, you were looked upon as the Brad Pitt of the college. Even though I looked more like Yul Brynner by then, I couldn't wait for my time to come! I had to wait a while.

Since I needed to establish myself in the college team, I ended up playing most weekends for Glamorgan Wanderers Youth. I was still eligible to play youth rugby but during that period I managed to have three games for the Wanderer's first team, which was quite a big deal at the time as they were in the so called 'Merit Table' of clubs: the top tier of Welsh rugby in those days.

My first game for the seniors was against Clifton. The report in the *Western Mail* the following Monday mentioned how this 'auburn haired giant (which was a bit of a laugh because by now my 'auburn hair' had been reduced to a very wide centre parting and a few strands down the sides!) had kicked Clifton off the park with his massive touch finders.'

Not a bad introduction to grown-up rugby if I do say so myself.

In my second year I began to establish myself in the college set up and I finally got picked for the college second team. I made my debut as an outside-half and pretty soon after I got into the first team. I was a predominately kicking outside-half whose first and second thoughts were always to kick, and then maybe to run the ball only if there was nowhere to boot the ball to. After a few games, Leighton Davies, the legendary coach and lecturer at the college, pulled me to one side. "Philip," he said, "you will never make an outside half as long as you have got a hole in your arse. I suggest you switch to full-back."

His frank assessment floored me. No one had spoken to me like that before. No one had been so brutally honest. I had always held my own, now I was being told I wasn't good enough. Was he wrong or was it me? The college was known throughout the country for its running rugby and to be honest it needed to be. It had become an essential part of the team's make-up. When playing the likes of Neath, Pontypool and Cardiff, a bunch of fit, young bum-fluffed students were never going to match the physical presence of those kinds of teams. The players for these established teams, especially the forwards, would be biting the heads off bats before the game, so the college's philosophy was run, run and run some more and I simply didn't fit in to that way of thinking.

I had to adapt or get left behind. Rather reluctantly, yet fortunately, I switched to full-back and it was as if someone had switched a light on for me and I had stepped out from the darkness. I discovered I had more time, more space and, believe it or not, I discovered that I did have a pair of legs which could be used to actually run. From that point on Forrest Gump had nothing on me!

College proved to be a brilliant time for me. Looking back now it was the happiest time of my life and the best rugby I ever played. We were all fit. In fact, we were probably the first professional outfit in Wales. Professional in as far as we trained all day. Our 'day job' was getting fit, playing rugby, watching what we ate, studying games on a big screen and, of course, the occasional lecture thrown in from time to time. Life consisted of sleeping, training, athletics, gym work and even dance sessions.

Although we were professional in our approach, the game was totally amateur yet I wouldn't swap those times for all the tea in China. Even in my free time, I found myself training. Heading for the gym to do weights or off down to the track for a run. There was always someone who wanted to do something. I loved it. It was like being in paradise for me.

Our philosophy and attitude to rugby was different to most of the other teams we played, mainly because we were a lot fitter. We'd run most teams off the park, especially the second class sides. Most of these teams were full of old heads, who liked to put the ball up the jumper. I recall one such game against Bedwas. They actually still talk about the game now in Bedwas Rugby Club if ever I go back there to report for the BBC or to speak at functions. They kicked off and we ran the ball from our own line and scored a try. They kicked off again and the same thing happened. Three times on the bounce we scored without them touching the ball other than restarting. We could tell they weren't amused. I think if we had done it for a fourth time, they would have just beaten us up. It was real heads-up rugby: a bit like how the French team used to play before the modern era.

The South Wales Police versus South Glamorgan Institute matches were always interesting fixtures, especially on the rare occasions when we won. It felt as if the police were out to nail a student and we were out put one over on a copper. They acted as if we were all dope smoking, layabouts. There was nothing further from the truth but try telling that to a copper trying to boot your head into touch.

Our fixtures saw us playing a mixture of first and second class sides. There's no such thing as a friendly in rugby and those guys didn't want a gang of fit, fresh-faced upstarts waltzing past them. Often it became a case of guerrilla warfare – real no holds barred rugby. Factory or pit workers, who had probably done more physical work in one shift than all of us put together had done in a year, but it proved to be a fantastic environment to learn the craft of the sport.

In my final year, our back division was almost exclusively Welsh speaking, well except for yours truly. To confuse the opposition all our set moves on the pitch were called in Welsh. Being a good old Cardiff boy of Irish Catholic stock, I was completely confused for most of the time. Not only did none of the other teams know what was about to happen, more often than not, neither did I, and I nearly always got it wrong. I'd go right and the ball would go left. They would call a 'miss one' and I would set up for a 'miss two'. Watching from the side-lines people must have thought I was a right idiot. And on occasions that's how I felt.

However, I must have impressed someone because I ended up playing for the Wales Colleges XV, then the British Colleges XV and was also selected for the Wales Students squad.

The most memorable match for South Glamorgan Institute was in my fourth year, playing Pontypool in the fourth round of the WRU Cup. The Cup was a massive competition in those days which often saw the so called second class clubs, 'the minnows', pit themselves against the top clubs.

Pontypool were consistently among the best teams, not

just in Wales but in the whole of the British Isles at that point in time. They were the Manchester United of Welsh rugby (although many said they looked and acted on occasions more like a team from the prison in the same city, Strangeways). They had an all-star cast with the famous 'Pontypool Front Row' as well as big hitters, in more ways than one, all over the park. To me it was a remarkable game of rugby.

Under instructions from the legendary coach Ray Prosser, they kept it tight. It was a real game of two completely contrasting styles and cultures. In the scrums, our eight went backwards at a rate of knots. The Pontypool pack was like eight human bulldozers. Even under all that pressure, we only ended up losing 28-8 and matched them two tries apiece, running the ball at every opportunity. That game more than any other I played in, summed up college rugby to me. Beauty versus the beast.

Off the field, it wasn't quite all train, train and train some more. There was more to college life than drinking pop and orange and doing press-ups. We could party as well as any team.

It was quite a unique experience playing in a team with your mates. Buddies who I spent most of my time with every day, very much like professional teams do today. We also knew each other pretty well. After most games we used to play some bizarre drinking games. One of the favourites was called five by five, or six by six or seven by seven. This simply meant you had to neck five pints by 5pm or six by 6pm and so on. The tipple of choice was always Strongbow. Of course, what else would students drink? It was cheap and got the job done quicker than most other drinks. The night always ended in a big sing-song.

It was during those fun-packed after match festivities that I first realised I could hold the attention of an audience. I didn't know what it was but I had something. I think it helped that I had a knack of remembering all the words to songs (no matter how 'Strongbowed-up' I was). I seemed to also make people laugh and had an ability to get them involved. I could ad-lib funny lines, was good at thinking on my feet and the more I stood in the spotlight, the happier I was.

I soon progressed to becoming the compère of the student variety shows. A big honour indeed.

In my third year, the college first team headed off to Berlin on a short tour to play the British Army of the Rhine XV. That trip proved to be a real eye-opener. It was still in the days when Germany was split between East and West and we had to go through Checkpoint Charlie to get into East Berlin. That was special but scary. I remember the silence as we slowly passed through the lines of straight-faced soldiers at the crossing point. No one said a word. Even I struggled at that moment to see the funny side of it. My heart was beating wildly in my chest, even though I had done nothing wrong. The dark cloud of oppression seemed to hang over the place and made us feel like we would be arrested at any moment.

We played at a ground, known as the Maifeld, next to the Olympic Stadium made famous by Jesse Owens winning four gold medals in front of Hitler at the Berlin Olympics of 1936. We got to stay in the officer's mess which was great because the drink was very cheap and the food plentiful.

Wherever and whenever I found myself on tour, I always went to Mass – another example of my 'A' level in 'Guilt' kicking in – so the soldiers arranged for a mini-bus to pick me up on the Sunday evening at the army barracks. I sat all alone on the bus. It must have appeared odd because a few hours earlier, I had been the livewire up on the stage but now I was sitting in the pews amongst a gaggle of old women making my peace with God in a language I didn't understand. None of my team mates said anything about me going, they just accepted it, but they must have been a little perplexed by it all.

On our last night someone invented the Quarter Past Four Club, which meant no one – and that meant no one – ventured to bed before 4.15am. Drinking strong German beer and singing at the top of our voices proved a great combination in those early hours and I was on top form. It definitely didn't seem like such a good idea when our bus picked us up an hour later to head back home to sunny Wales. You should have seen the state on us all boarding the coach. It was the journey from hell!

At the end of my third year I got my degree – a BA (Honours) in Human Movement Studies – graded as a 2:2 or, in student parlance, a 'Desmond', as in Archbishop Desmond Tutu.

As I headed into my fourth and final year it was time to decide which postgraduate course I wished to take. To be honest it wasn't a difficult decision at all as I'd always wanted to get a Postgraduate Certificate in Education (PGCE) and become a PE teacher. So that last year, and especially those final few months, really started to focus the mind.

During the holiday before starting my final year I went home to Ely to play for Glamorgan Wanderers. The first day of the season, we beat Cardiff 15-9 at the Arms Park – the first time the Wanderers had ever beaten their near neighbours. It was an emotional night! the president of Glamorgan Wanderers was World War Two hero Sir Tasker Watkins VC, who would go on to become president of the Welsh Rugby Union. I saw the tears of joy in his eyes in the changing room after the match and I then realised that there was a lot more to rugby than 30 men chasing a ball for their own enjoyment. It wasn't about the individual, but the team and the supporters and that strong feeling of belonging to a club. Real rugby, and any real team sport is about the players and fans being a 'band of brothers'!

In my final year, part of the training meant going into schools to see how teachers and schools in the real world operated, and I can tell you that entering a classroom full of kids for the first time certainly concentrates the mind. It really brought home to me that at the end of term I would be packing up my bags, taking off my treasured green tracksuit and heading out as a real teacher, in real schools, with real kids. The security of college life would be removed.

With this in mind, the first thing I needed was to secure a teaching post or risk being an ex-student signing on the dole! Facing the prospect of life on the breadline, I changed. I realised that college life was coming to an end. Like the last scene in the movie, *St Elmo's Fire*, when the old gang look through the window of their regular college bar only to see their old haunt being occupied by a new bunch of upstarts. That's the circle of college life I guess. Life moves on. You have got to move on with it.

At the end of the season we had a rugby tour to America. We stayed in the Allentown area of Pennsylvania, made famous by the Billy Joel song. We played against some decent American college teams and a couple of local clubs. It was in the States that the Yanks gave me another, rather harsh, nickname. For my final tour with South Glamorgan Institute I was now 'Ladle Head'.

My final game for the college whilst on that tour proved to be quite an emotional affair and my last night as a student drinking in the college bar in June 1983 will stay with me forever. To witness a gang of so-called, big, strong rugby players all sobbing is not a sight you see every day. The more drink that flowed, the more crying took place.

Those four years in Cyncoed were the best of my life. I'd made some great friends, several of who went on to make a name for themselves in the sporting world. People like Kevin Hopkins – still today my closest friend – who went on to play for Wales,

Rhodri Lewis who was capped whilst at college, international cricketers Greg Thomas and Hugh Morris and a host of other very good club players who not only went on to play top class rugby but who also became superb teachers and coaches.

The bonds of friendship you develop at college are binding for life. Kevin Hopkins was my best man when I remarried a couple of years ago, as I had been for him at his wedding in 1991.

My other great mates were Marc Batten, Terry Jones, Huw Gilson, Gareth Francis, Darryl Richards and John Morgan. It says a lot about our friendship that when tragedy stuck my life in 2009 these six lads came *en bloc* from all parts of the country to make sure I was alright.

In those four years I don't remember ever having a bout of depression. I'm not sure if it was because I was busy all the time, out socialising and enjoying my rugby but I never had a problem.

Looking back to those years it's made me think, whether that is the missing part of the jigsaw when someone suffers from depression. Is there a need for that person to be doing things they love – as much as possible – to prevent their mind from drifting off to a place where they are imprisoned inside their own head with only their own thoughts for company? Paul Gascoigne is probably a fine example of someone who has suffered from this. Paul was a footballing genius, yet a man who couldn't control the demons buzzing around his own mind. If he could have played football for 24 hours a day, seven days a week until he was well into his old age, would he have been a different person to the one he became? Would he still be the Paul Gascoigne the public loved? I'm not sure.

But depression was nowhere to be seen for me. I was more than happy and everything seemed to be on the up.

During every holiday period whilst at college, instead of

lazing about and watching TV I always got a holiday job as I needed to pay my way. I'm glad I did though, as it really grounded me. The experience stood me in good stead for the real world, the adult world which I was about to enter. People have always commented on how down to earth I am. I don't think that was only to do with my upbringing, but also with the jobs I had during my college years. I worked with a soft drinks, wine and spirits company delivering to all the Co-op shops throughout the valleys. Virtually every village in Wales had a Co-op store then, so I did a lot of travelling.

I got to know the valleys like the back of my hand. Being a Cardiff boy it seemed like a different country to me. Not just the scenery, which was beautiful, but the culture, the people, and their sense of humour. I met some great characters – really honest, down to earth people.

Being one of the college's sporting, shining lights, my trips up the valleys proved to be a great leveller compared to college where an unwritten hierarchy was, and probably still is, an accepted part of student life. The first year students look up to the fourth years as if they were gods. Even today if I became the most powerful man in the world, I would still be in awe of Kevin Edwards, who was one of the stars of the college team when I was a first year 'pup'. Even now Hugh Morris, ex-England cricket and chief executive of Glamorgan cricket club still speaks to me with the kind of respect reserved for one's elders. That is because I was one of the college rugby stars when he was a young freshman.

However, all that 'puppy love' college admiration was forgotten when I was out on the pop lorry. The job was definitely a way of keeping my feet firmly on the ground. I wasn't the big cheese in this arena that I was back in college. Here, I was the young delivery lad, having the mickey taken out of me all the time.

There was one guy who worked in the company, Ray Palfrey, who I'll never forget as he was such a natural comedian. Subconsciously I think I may have modelled myself on him, or tried to, in later years. He was the star turn 24/7. Always smiling, always cracking jokes or singing. He could use a swear word as a noun, verb or adjective. His swearing was terrible but he wasn't offensive and the expletives coming from Ray almost sounded like poetry. I used to idolize him and I loved to be in his company. Gareth Edwards, rugby superstar, and Ray Palfrey from Cilfynydd were my two heroes as a young man. He would drive around in his forklift truck, singing his heart out with a pretend microphone. On one occasion he was operating the machine with one hand and singing some Tom Jones number into a bottle of pop held in the other. Unexpectedly he lost control and smashed into a stack of pallets of fizzy drinks. The bottles exploded and there was a bubbling sea of lemonade and orangeade everywhere.

I've never forgotten the humour he brought to our workplace. He used to lift my spirits every morning and I learnt a lot from him. He unlocked the everyday humour gene inside me. His motto was 'not to take life too seriously', which is an outlook I adopted. That must sound odd coming from a bloke who'd go on to suffer from severe depression but that's what I tried to do. He was worth his weight in gold to me. Those summer and Christmas jobs smoothed the edges off me and tempered any youthful arrogance I might have had. I've always tried to respect people no matter what they do, or don't do, in life. To me the holiday job was a short-term way of earning some cash but, to the valley people I came across, this was their lives, this was what they did for a living; day-in, day-out. I will never forget that.

It was during my final year that I met Liz. It was just before New Year's Eve in 1982 and I was out with my cricket mate,

Mal Morgan, who she worked with. I thought not only was she beautiful, but she had the most wonderful laugh. I'm not sure if she was just being polite or if she really found me that funny but every time I opened my mouth, I made her laugh. I was in my element, on top form, with this beautiful person as my one-woman audience.

Liz Godfrey lived in Llanishen. Her late grandfather had owned Godfrey's Garages, a well-known car dealership in Cardiff. Being a good Ely boy my aim was to always marry into a bit of money and to become a kept man!!! But seriously, I knew within two weeks she was the one I wanted to spend the rest of my life with. I liked everything about her. She just ticked all the right boxes for me. Better still, her family were great to me and Liz got on with mine. To this day I still refer to Liz's mother Judith as 'Mum'.

Liz's father, Malcolm, had died a few years before we met and that had a profound effect on her. She told me how she couldn't, or didn't want to get close to anyone for a long time. His death had made her put up a defensive wall around herself and although we both knew we liked each other she kept her innermost feelings at arm's length, until one night in a skittle alley. We were in the Glamorgan Wanderers rugby club having a game of skittles when, after bowling, she turned to me and said, "I want to tell you that I do."

"Do what?" I could hardly hear her over the noise.

"I do love you."

"Oh that's good," I replied over the deafening din of rolling balls, clattering wood and bawdy cheering.

It wasn't a 'Romeo and Juliet on the balcony' moment. It was a 'skittle alley in Cardiff' moment, but it was the best moment ever. It had taken her a long time to finally get close to someone again. Luckily for me, I had been the one to help lower the armour she had wrapped around herself.

52

Everything clicked between us. As they say, our stars just aligned.

I left college in July 1983 as a fully qualified teacher. Now the real work began. In the August I got my first proper teaching assignment at Blaengwawr Comprehensive School in Aberdare. To celebrate, that summer Liz and I holidayed in Little Haven in Pembrokeshire. We had such a wonderful time there that it became our special place. A place we would cherish always. I felt so happy. I was about to start my first job, I was planning my wedding to the loveliest girlfriend I could imagine plus my rugby future looked bright as several clubs had showed more than a passing interest in me playing for them.

A new era was beginning for me. The world was my oyster and by the September of 1983, if I could have bottled and sold the confidence running through my veins, I would have been a millionaire, and the happiest man in the world. I'd even made my first half-century during that summer's cricket season. It was my year, I was flying. Depression...what depression?

I loved the valleys, the humour, the people and sense of community which we didn't always have in Cardiff. I'd had a little experience of valleys life whilst delivering pop but this was another world altogether and to be honest, stepping into a comprehensive school in those days was damn scary.

The kids would say, "Der Sir...you don't come from Cardiff do you?" I would nod in reply. "What's it like?" they'd ask. It was said in a way as if it was a place that was a million miles away instead of just half an hour by car.

The post was primarily teaching PE but the contract meant I also had to teach French to two form one classes – well I did have an 'O' level in it! Hence, here were these kids in a school in Aberdare getting taught French by a boy from Ely. When I entered the classroom the conversation would go something like this:

"Bonn Jaw Toot La Mond."

"Bonsure Miss you're Steele."

"Ok class...get your books out."

I really did wing it as I went along. I didn't know what the hell I was doing. Hopefully the kids didn't notice too much and more importantly, I hope they learned a little from my pigeon French lessons.

When I came out of college, probably like most teachers, I had a dream I was going to change the world. I was going to be the greatest PE teacher that's ever walked the earth. I was going to coach the school team to cup final wins ever year. I would get all my players capped by Wales in every sport possible: rugby, cricket, football, table tennis, and tiddly-winks. Maybe even get voted best teacher that's ever been! But reality is a whole different ball game. Never mind winning cup finals, if I could actually get 20 out of the 30 boys in the class to bring their PE kit to school that was a major success.

I don't want this to come across harshly against the kids or the valleys. I loved teaching in the school and I loved the kids, but what you learn in text books or hours upon hours of lectures could never prepare you for the reality of dealing with the wants and needs of a class of children.

The notes from parents excusing their sons from PE lessons were priceless. I could write a book on those alone, featuring gems such as:

Dear Mr Steele,
Please could David be excused from PE today as last night he fell over and bruised his cock sick in the bottom of his back.

and

THE COLLEGE OF KNOWLEDGE

Peter can't do Jim today cos he snot well. Please will you execute him Mr Steele.

I'm not just saying this but I did love every minute of it. In those two years I met three of the greatest friends I could ever wish to have – Peter Ford, Phil Rees and Mike Thomas – and we're still friends to this day. We had so many great laughs. They brought so much wit to the workplace and, let me tell you, at times we needed a good sense of humour in the staff room, just to see us through each day.

Peter was in charge of the partial hearing class. One of the kids, a super boy, was deaf in one ear. He was a hard working lad and on the rugby field he was a real grafter.

All the valley kids started their sentence with "Der Sir...what are we doing today." However this partially deaf kid couldn't say his 'Ss'. He would wander in to the changing room, shirt normally hanging out, and say, "Der, Dir" or "Dir, Der."

Because of his strong Valley accent and his speech impairment, I didn't know what was the 'der' and what was the 'sir' part. I would just nod at him and tell him to get changed. He was such a smashing kid and a good rugby player.

I always seemed to get on better with the kids with special educational needs. It's not text book stuff. It's real. I got on better with the more challenging kids, those who were perceived to be not as bright as 'normal' kids in the educational system. Many of those 'more challenging' kids are now a lot more successful than most of the 'normal' kids have ever been.

Being a full-time sports teacher (with a *petit* bit of French thrown in for good measure) was also a great way to stay in shape to play rugby. Lots of guys playing first class rugby in those days had proper jobs. 'Spikey' Watkins, for example, the captain of Newport and later Wales, earned a living driving a 16-tonne truck for 10 hours a day. Others worked down the mines, or in factories. At least I was lucky enough to be doing something I loved, being out in the fresh air and getting exercise. Some days, if the weather was bad (and it often was in Aberdare) I would go on three cross-country runs with different classes in one day. Being fit really helped my confidence.

I still had no doubts, or demons or depression clouds floating over me. I settled into the job straight away. In my mind I was a natural. I could have taken on the world, and won.

One of the toughest yet most enlightening periods of my teaching career was during the Miners' Strike of 1984-85. The valleys during that troubled time became a war zone. When I was in college I didn't really care about politics or what was happening in the real world. Finance and grown-up stuff like that didn't interest me. There were only three things that mattered to me, sport, sport and more sport. I just focused on becoming good enough to win a Welsh cap. That was always my goal, my dream. I didn't care which political party was in power and, as I was from Ely, a predominantly Labour area anyway, there didn't seem to be much point in voting. Being in college took me a million miles away from reality in lots of ways. Like lots of 21-year-olds, there were more important things in life than listening to an old bloke in a suit and tie. Politics had nothing to do with me.

The miner's strike switched a light bulb on in my head. To see whole communities destroyed and ripped to pieces was devastating. To see those poor kids in the school struggling to survive during that unrest, which at times resembled a civil war, was painful. It made me think of things more deeply. Probably for the first time in my life I considered the bigger issues outside of my own little bubble – social, political and economic issues.

I had been brought up in a Catholic world where you didn't really question authority and the social order. We were given the bible and told that it explained how everything happened – what was good and what was evil – and told to accept it. The mindset was to keep your head down and pray for redemption. My upbringing – a good family, a good education, a college degree, successful at sport and great mates – meant I'd been shielded from the harsher world experienced by many others in Wales and beyond. I didn't know what it was like to feel real grinding hardship. Aberdare, like most valley mining towns, seemed to be in the eye of the destructive hurricane that was the Miners' Strike. Many of our pupils had fathers who worked at the Phurnacite coking plant in Abercwmboi, which produced smokeless fuel from coal and was a huge employer in the valley. Almost overnight, the impact of the strike was plain to see with many children switching to free school meals as their fathers' incomes vanished. What really hit me was when when one kid came to PE and said he couldn't do games because he didn't have any togs or boots to wear. "Sir, my father works at the Phurnacite and he's on strike. He said to tell you we can't afford food never mind football boots."

The honesty in his words hit me like a baseball bat across the head. Four years of college didn't prepared me for something like that. No text book in the world could ever describe the look on that poor boy's face. It was heart-breaking.

Driving home each night I'd see people on street corners holding out collection buckets or asking for cans of food. It was like a third world country, in my own country. What was going on? I didn't understand it. I went to a 'Miners' Benefit' concert organised by a Cardiff folk-singer named Dave Burns. It was a night of protest songs and it was amazing. As I sat there and listened to the words of the songs about the struggles of the downtrodden and oppressed it kick-started an interest and love of folk music that I've kept to this day.

It was around about this time that, together with my

brother John I started to learn the guitar. I'd always loved the sound of the acoustic guitar ever since hearing Ralph McTell's *Streets of London* which made the charts in 1974. With the help of my teaching colleague Peter Ford – who showed me a few chords and rhythms – along with lots of practise, I was able to pick it up quite quickly. Rather than just learning and practising chords which can be laborious, I learned songs. I soon discovered that I had a knack of being able to learn and remember lyrics, even to very long, narrative ballads.

I soon became a big fan of folk music and singers like Ralph McTell, Gordon Lightfoot, The Dubliners, The Fureys, Tom Paxton and Christy Moore. Strangely enough I got to interview Ralph McTell on a programme I was presenting for BBC Radio Wales called *Extra Time*. Even more strange was the fact that the interview was all about his love of rugby (he is a friend of legendary former Wales and Lions full-back JPR Williams) and nothing to do with music whatsoever.

I've also always been a big fan of two very talented Welsh musicians – Frank Hennessy and Mal Pope. In my opinion they are two of Wales' most underestimated talents both as performers and broadcasters. They are also two fantastic guys who have always been generous with their support and encouragement during my career. A couple of years back, when I used to do a regular spot reading the Saturday morning sports bulletins on Radio Wales, I would always take my guitar into the studio on the last weekend before Christmas and join Mal in a duet of Shane MacGowan's *Fairy Tale of New York* on his early morning show. I'm not sure I've ever heard Huw Edwards or John Humphrys do the same!

For a couple of years I fronted a folk band named a Celtic Air, which included my brother John and a few friends – Phil Turner, Mark Heron and Mark Edmonds. We played quite a few gigs around south Wales until it became more difficult to find the time to practise together.

These days I play occasionally at folk clubs and sometimes as part of an after-dinner speech if it's appropriate, but I still try to make time to practise or learn new songs virtually every day.

The whole Miner's Strike episode opened my eyes and I began to appreciate there was more to life than playing sport. I quickly started to learn about politics and to realise rugby was only a game. It was distressing to see how the heart and soul had been ripped out of the community. The government had waged war on hard working innocent people and was breaking their lives apart.

Compared to the sadness I felt for those people, everything in my own life was still going well. I felt no personal sense of doom. I couldn't even see a cliff never mind totter on the edge of it. In fact, perhaps things were going too well!

4

In a 'Newport State of Mind'

'Phil was an impressive player at Cardiff's Cyncoed college in the early 1980s so when he graduated I, as club captain, invited him join Newport RFC. He was quite a nervous young man and eager to quickly impress our coach, Charlie Faulkner, so when we met up for pre-season training he tried to strike up a conversation by asking about his choice of boots. "Are those spikes you're wearing tonight Charlie?" Phil asked, to which Charlie snapped back, "No, you cheeky bastard, they're mine." I think Phil thought he had messed up before he even started with Newport but we all laughed it off, except for Charlie who kept on for weeks about that "cheeky college boy"! It was always a pleasure captaining teams with Phil in the side and knowing him as a genuinely lovely person who needed managing in a certain way to get the best out of him as a rugby player.'

Mike 'Spikey' Watkins
Wales

In the summer of 1983, everything looked rosy in my own little garden. I'd got the job at the school in Aberdare and I was now engaged to Liz. However, as far as the rugby was concerned, I knew that to be taken seriously and to progress my playing career, I had to go and make my mark playing for one of the perceived bigger clubs of Welsh rugby. It was time to go and perform at a higher level, week-in and week-out.

Cardiff asked me to go and train with them, and being a Cardiff boy – and still living in the city – the capital-based team seemed like the obvious choice. But that all changed on a sunny Sunday afternoon in June whilst playing cricket for my club Wenvoe up in Abercarn in the heart of the beautiful Gwent valleys.

While standing out near the boundary, I noticed a stocky but athletic looking guy, wearing red tracksuit bottoms and a T-shirt, making a beeline towards me from the fields opposite. Even before he got to me I could tell from a distance he was a 'somebody'. He had an air about him. When he came closer I recognised the 'somebody' was no other than Mike 'Spikey' Watkins, the captain of Newport RFC.

"How's it going Phil?" he asked.

His words took me by surprise since I didn't realise he knew who I was.

"What are you doing next season?" he quickly added.

"I'm not sure yet Spike," I replied, trying to keep one eye on the cricket match going on in front of me.

"Why don't you come and join us at Newport. We've been watching you for a while and we could do with some good backs like you."

I was some-what taken-aback. I'd played against Newport for the college once or twice, which usually ended with us getting hammered by 50 points or more. All I remembered doing in those games was tackling, catching high balls and lining up behind our posts while they took numerous conversions. Considering that, I was pleased he had seen some potential in me. I'm not sure if he had purposely targeted me that day or if he had just been running past and saw an opportunity. Whatever it was, even him just knowing me, made me feel a million dollars. Me, a 22-year-old, being asked to go and play for a famous club like Newport by a legend such as 'Spikey' Watkins was an honour. He had been one of my idols when he played for Cardiff in the late 1970s, when I was one of the club's ball boys.

It was still hard to believe that all of a sudden I had been asked to go and train with two of the biggest club sides in the world. I went along to both but against all the odds and everyone else's advice, I decided to go with Newport. In a nutshell, I felt the club had been more welcoming than their great rivals. I hadn't really felt that comfortable whilst training with Cardiff. I found it a bit impersonal.

Newport on the other hand greeted me with open arms. We trained at St. Julian's High School, where 'Spikey' and the coach, the legendary Charlie Faulkner – the former Wales and Lions prop – made a big fuss of me, shaking my hand and thanking me for coming down. They made me feel special and wanted. It seemed more like a family than a club.

I made my mind up quite quickly my rugby future lay with Newport and informed Glamorgan Wanderers of my decision. To be fair there were no hard feelings. They were happy that I was moving up in my career.

I was fit before going to Newport but their training methods were something else. They were basic and brutal to say the least. The sessions transpired to be very regimental and extremely tough. They always started at 7pm and that meant 7pm exactly, not 7.01pm or we'd get a right old bollocking. Most sessions consisted of lots and lots of running and physical contact. Up hills, down hills, and then back up the hills. There always seemed to be more going up than coming down.

As the season approached, Charlie would always have us playing 'unopposed' games – the in-joke was we did that for practice for when we played Penarth. Yet to be honest, most or nearly all of it consisted of the forwards having the ball. The backline hardly had a sniff for the entire session.

After another rather forward dominated session, Charlie sidled up to me and muttered, "Oh Steeley...you're from that college of knowledge, what do you think of our style of play?"

"Charlie" I replied, "the forward play is brilliant. You are an absolute scientist when it comes to the pack, but when do the backs get the ball?"

"In f*****g April," he grunted, and stomped off.

Nevertheless, Newport was building a good team and I was looking forward to the start of the new season. Up to that point in my playing career I'd never struggled with any kind of injury, I guess I'd been extremely lucky, but that was all about to change. Pre-season had been great. I felt fit and confident and happy I had made the right move. Then in our final trial match I got tackled by Roger Powell, a no-nonsense flanker, and I ended up springing my collar bone. After all that effort and hard work I'd put in, it meant I couldn't make my debut in the first game of the season. I was gutted.

During my time playing college rugby and even to an extent with Glamorgan Wanderers, the games varied quite a bit as far as toughness was concerned. One game we would be facing one of the top sides but then we could have three or four games against easier opposition. At Newport, every game was hard. If my memory serves me right, in my first season we kicked off the campaign with a friendly against Pill Harriers (some friendly that was!!) then Bristol (like World War One), Swansea, Pontypool (World War Two and Three combined), Cardiff, Llanelli, Neath and then the Barbarians. It doesn't get much tougher than that I guess. When I played for the college we would be lucky to play one or two top class sides in a month. Now it was like playing six cup finals in three weeks.

It was clear I'd entered a new level of rugby altogether. Not just like a cup final, but a hard, no holds barred cup final, played in front of passionate and often fanatical fans. Running out onto an away pitch was like entering a Roman amphitheatre dressed as a Christian. The tribalism in Welsh rugby was unbelievable. Also, when playing for the college team, we really weren't expected to win against the big boys and we rarely did. There was seldom the aggression and violence towards us that lurked in rugby in those good old, bad old days. It was all, 'Fair play, *chwarae teg*. You students had a good go', or something along those lines! I soon found out that, for many teams, playing against Newport was akin to waving a red rag to a raging bull. I could feel the hatred and taste the aggression in the crowd's chants. They would spit and shout, and bay for blood. Often I felt sorry for the referees. They only came to ref a decent game of rugby and often they must have felt like peace envoys or policeman in a street brawl.

Apart from my little injury everything started off well for me and, during one of our first games, against Swansea, I scored a try. The best thing was that it was televised and I ran through the Welsh full-back at the time, Mark Wyatt, to touch down. That helped my confidence no end.

Next up came the big one. I always knew the rivalry between Cardiff and Newport was massive – as it was down west between the likes of Swansea and Llanelli and in later years, Neath – but I never appreciated just how colossal the Pontypool v Newport games were. It was probably the biggest of the lot. No disrespect to Ebbw Vale but these were the two top dogs in Gwent squaring up to each other. Pontypool had been the kingpins for many a year and now 'Spikey' and his warriors from Newport were looking to take their crown.

To put it mildly, 'Spikey' – our captain – wasn't everyone's cup of tea but I loved him. He was infamous both on and off the field for his antics but he definitely had a rare gift. He was just the sort of captain a player like me needed. He was not only a great player himself, as hard as nails, but also a brilliant motivator and I'm certain that even a pacifist would march off to war after one of his team talks. Players would run through brick walls for him. Not many people I have met before or since possessed that ability.

In the changing rooms before the Pooler game, he'd pace about, with his shirt collar tucked in to his jersey and Vaseline like varnish coating his face. That was his war paint – Geronimo Watkins.

He started off quite quiet and controlled. "Boys...boys." He looked at everyone in turn. It was pure theatre. A cross between a battle cry and the best parts of a Shakespeare play. There was complete silence in the room. My heart was beating hard against my chest as I sat in the corner. "No one can beat us boys," he added. He then went around everyone in turn. "Steeley," he looked me in the eye, "I know you are the best full-back in Wales...now let's go and show them what you can do."

Tension crept up the walls; aggression oozing out of everyone's pores. The whole team gathered in a huddle and punched the air ten times. A few forwards punched the walls and then each other. I made sure I wasn't standing near to any of them. It was madness. Half the team appeared bruised and battered and we hadn't even started the game yet.

"Are we ready?" 'Spikey' roared.

"Yes!" we all roared back.

"I can't hear you. Are we ready?" It was like a rock concert with 'Spikey' on stage whipping the audience into a frenzy.

"YEEEEEES!!"

We all raced out of the changing rooms as if we were going over the trenches to fight the Germans in no-man's land, but that's when it got rather surreal. The changing rooms at

65

Newport in those days were about 200 yards from the ground. What a weird sensation from leaving the intense pressure cooker environment of the changing rooms to rushing out into the relative calm and sunshine of a park on a September evening. As we jogged across to the stadium I could hear and almost feel the atmosphere inside. Running out on the field that day will stay with me forever. The chants of 'Newport' and 'Pooler' greeted us. The noise was deafening with over 10,000 fans squeezed tightly into Rodney Parade. It was by far the biggest crowd I'd ever played in front of. Like walking into the classroom for the first time, this was something I hadn't been prepared for.

Then another surreal moment greeted us. We had a minute's silence for a great guy named Terry Morgan, who had suffered serious neck injury playing for Abertillery a few seasons before and had tragically died the week of our game. Both teams faced up to each other. I looked across at the line of Pontypool players glaring back at us: Graham Price, Jeff Squire, Eddie Butler, Steve Sutton, David Bishop, Chris Huish, Staff Jones, Steve Jones, John Perkins and the rest. I almost felt like I should have brought my autograph book onto the pitch with me! These were the original wild bunch but a wild bunch that could play a bit of rugby as well.

Mind you, under 'Spikey', our pack of forwards were no angels. He and Charlie had purposely put together a set of guys that could not only stand up in the face of intimidation, but could well and truly dish it out as well.

At the first line out, 'Spikey' threw the ball in and then all hell broke loose. Perkins smacked our second row David 'Dai' Waters, 'Spikey' smacked Steve Jones and Roger Powell smacked everyone in sight. We may as well have left the ball in the changing rooms for the first five minutes, as the fists and the boots rained in from all angles. The crowd loved it.

I stood at full-back watching it all. I turned to my wing Marc Batten, who had joined Newport with me from college and muttered, "I don't think we're in Kansas anymore Toto."

If I'd been wearing a pair of ruby slippers instead of Patrick rugby boots, I would have clicked them together and got the hell out of there.

We lost the game. In truth their pack was just too strong for us. On saying that, I think I had a reasonably good game. You know, when you play against Pontypool, you're going to have to make a lot of tackles and catch lots of high balls. At times it felt like being centre stage in one of those David Attenborough wildlife films with herds of rhino, elephants and wildebeest thundering down on me. There I was, waiting for the ball to drop from the heavens while their entire pack sprinted towards me, steam coming out of their ears, snarls on their faces and studs in their boots ready for some stamping.

I stood my ground even though I got trampled many times and I think I earned myself a bit of respect from the players and fans alike. It was lucky that I had no hair by then as, with the kicking my head had taken, I wouldn't have been able to use a comb for a week.

After the game our changing room looked like the A&E department at the local hospital. We were all gutted we had lost but as they say, you have to take it on the chin, take the count and learn from the experience.

As the weeks progressed, it proved not to be the last beating we'd suffer but we were definitely getting better. The 'Spike' Watkins mantra was, "No one can beat us, we can only beat ourselves."

He wasn't far wrong. We lost a couple of games because we'd been sloppy and given the ball away or conceded a silly late penalty or were trying too hard. He also said, "One of these days we are going to give someone a right bollocking."

That day came a few games later when we beat Cardiff 35-20 at Rodney Parade – a record score at that time.

I remember an old fan coming up to me after the game. "Well done young Steele. I've been watching Newport since 1935 and I've seen us play Cardiff many times but that's the best I've ever seen Newport play." He was very emotional, with tears in his eyes. Nothing beats that feeling when you see the joy and happiness on the supporters' faces. We had just made that elderly gentleman's day, his week and perhaps his year – it was a real honour to be part of it.

Of course, being a Cardiff boy, it was also a strange experience for me – taking delight in beating my home town – but that is sport. I was Newport through and through by then, so much so that even today people who saw me play still ask me what part of Newport am I from?

I was enjoying my rugby and hearing people tell me that I'd gone from being a promising player to a very good player.

One of the matches I was looking forward to was against the Barbarians in October. I was so excited because I was finally going to play against, in my opinion, one of the greatest attacking full-backs, Andy Irving of Scotland and the Lions. As a running full-back he was an even bigger hero to me than JPR Williams. I know that is sacrilege for another Welshman to admit to that, but I loved everything Andy did. He could run like a stag and had a sidestep that could outfox MI5. However, on the morning of the game he pulled out because of an Achilles tendon injury. I was gutted but I had a half decent game. The report in the *Telegraph* said, 'The Barbarians' defence found increasing problems quelling the willowy Steele who twice surprised Rees with his acceleration.' That was Clive Rees, the Wales and Lions' winger – know 'Billy Whizz' – and one of the fastest in the game. I'm sure I still have that press cutting under my pillow!

Many years later, I played up in Edinburgh for an invitation Welsh Veterans Select XV against Scotland, on the morning of the Wales v Scotland game in 1995. I was hoping Andy Irving would be playing but he wasn't. In the evening there was a big gala dinner at which I gave the after-dinner speech. When I finished, Andy, who had been at the dinner, came over to thank me and tell me how much he'd enjoyed it.

"Oh," I joked, "I've a bone to pick with you" and then proceeded to tell him about the Barbarians game in Newport twelve years earlier and how I'd been disappointed after he'd dropped out. "It would have been one of my greatest ambitions to play against you," I added.

Without a seconds' hesitation he promised he would definitely come to Wales and play in the same fixture the following year and, to his credit, a year later, at Taff's Well RFC, the brilliant Andy Irving turned out for the Scottish Veterans XV against us. I tackled him once and when helping him up, I said, "Thanks so much for coming. You made my dream come true." A bit sloppy but it was so true. What a great bloke and a true gentleman.

Back at Newport I was really enjoying my rugby. We all were. We had a good side and my confidence was sky high. My performances must have alerted the powers-that-be because there was a little rumour I was on the radar of the Welsh selectors.

I couldn't believe it. If true, it would be the best news ever. Things really seemed to be getting better and better for me. In spite of this, I did have a small worry. For a few weeks I'd had a constant nagging pain in my groin. I got over it enough to play by taking anti-inflammatory pain-killing tablets. When the tablets kicked in, the pain would disappear for a while but soon come back with a vengeance.

It came to a head in a match against Tredegar. The pain got so bad I hobbled off and I was side-lined for a while. The next game for me was at Rosslyn Park. I survived it, just, but something was definitely not right – I could tell – yet I kept reassuring myself it would go away and everything would be fine.

Later that week, I was sat in my house listening intently to the 6.30pm Welsh news on the radio. Martyn Williams, the presenter, was about to announce the Wales B Squad for the fixture against France B later that month. I crossed my fingers and toes and said a little, sly prayer. I could hardly control myself on hearing my name being read out. The rumours had been true. I was in the squad. Myself and Bridgend's Howell Davies had been the two full backs selected.

In those days, playing for the Wales B team was quite a big deal. Often it proved a very useful stepping stone to get in the first team, especially since the main Welsh team were going through a very bad run. They had recently lost to Romania and had only narrowly beaten Japan. The senior team lacked confidence and fans were looking for changes to be made. I didn't want to think too far ahead – I was in dreamland already – and I hadn't been expecting the call up in the first place, so God only knows what could happen next. One good performance and I could be on the verge of winning a full Welsh cap. It was in my hands. I had to pinch myself to make sure I wasn't going to wake-up.

Another piece of positive news was that five other players from Newport, including 'Spikey' as the captain, had also got the nod. This was great because not only did the Wales B side need someone like 'Spikey' leading them, the whole of Wales needed a strong and committed character like him to help pull us out of the doldrums. We needed someone or something to galvanise an entire country.

A few days later, I received a letter through the door confirming my selection plus a form for me to sign for the

Adidas kit I was going to have. The Welsh Rugby Union had recently signed a deal with the sportswear firm which was now to supply their official kit. To say I was overjoyed would be an understatement. I couldn't stop smiling. Still, I knew my groin wasn't right and I didn't know what to do. It wasn't just a groin strain. I could sense it, feel it. To make sure I would be ok, and with the Wales B squad's first training session taking place at the Arms Park on the Sunday, I withdrew from Newport's Saturday game. I was desperate to be 'right'.

Nervous about my injury niggle, I spoke to 'Spikey' on the Saturday. I trusted him. He'd kept the bench warm for Bobby Windsor, as an unused replacement for the great Welsh team of the late 1970s, before being cast out into the wilderness for his off the field antics. He knew how the system worked.

"Spike," I said. "I can't train tomorrow, my groin is playing up."

He turned to me and with all his years of experience he said, "Listen Steeley, take a few of those pain-killing tablets (I was already taking 1800 milligrams of ibuprofen a day) run around a bit, pretend to pull something, come off, get your kit," and, as if to emphasise the point, he said it again; "get your kit," before adding "then have a bit of a rest and everything will be okay."

I knew he was right but with me having an 'A' level in 'Guilt', I couldn't do it. I knew it was dishonest. 'Thou shall not lie, even if it means seeing your dream get washed down the drain.'

I arrived at training and told the selectors I had a problem. I went to the medical room where two doctors checked me out. Both told me it was a groin strain and I would be out for three weeks, thus missing the France game. I had a degree in physical education and although I wasn't a medic I knew they were wrong. There was too much pain for a groin strain.

Dejectedly, I walked back to the training ground. I stood

71

there, heartbroken. I tried to hold it all together, but found it so hard. I couldn't talk to anyone. Something inside kept telling me it was all slipping away. I could see my big chance riding off into the distance in a big cloud of dust. I told myself it would probably be the only chance I would ever get. Lightening never strikes twice, or so they say.

Rod Morgan, one of the selectors, came up to me, "Sorry to hear about the injury Phil."

John Dawes, the WRU coaching organiser came up next, "Don't worry Phil, your time will come again."

Me, being the 'glass is half-empty' kind of person, doubted it would. I just stood on the touchline watching the squad go through the motions. I should have been out there enjoying it – enjoying the whole experience. I should have been running around with my new teammates and soaking up the atmosphere instead of standing there about to burst into tears.

With hindsight, maybe I should have been stronger. I can imagine what someone like Jonathan Davies, the brilliant outside-half, would have said if he had been in my shoes. He'd have quipped, 'Yeah, of course I will because I'm the best player about and I should be on the field, so I'll be back.'

Not me. I was the opposite. The doubts crept in. My new sense of confidence began disappearing down the drain. The training session ended and we all filed into a room to claim our expenses. I hadn't trained and since I lived in Cardiff anyway I didn't believe I should claim anything. The odd thing was that some players had no qualms about claiming, saying things like 'I've come here via my sick auntie's house in St. David's, that's a round-trip of 200 miles.' It sounded like some would say anything for a few quid extra. Whilst at first it sounded wrong, it wasn't long before I began to see it from their perspective, as I soon discovered that getting anything out of the WRU was like getting blood from a stone.

I walked into the room where all our kits were lined up. As we queued I could see my kit all packed neatly in cellophane wrapping. There was a tracksuit with the WRU feathers, an Adidas rainsuit, boots, training shirts and jumpers. My eyes were drawn to the feathers stitched on the tracksuit. I couldn't wait to put it on. A picture of me strolling down the street, looking 100 feet tall popped into my mind. I couldn't take my eyes off it. "That's mine," I whispered to myself.

The queue couldn't move quick enough for me. As I waited, John Dawes came up. "Phil...I don't know if you've heard but the chairman of selectors has said that only those who took part in training today can have the kit."

It felt like someone had put a gun to my head and fired. I physically wobbled. I think I said something like, "Ok...ok... John...I understand." What I should have said was, 'You bunch of tight-arsed bastards. I'd paid for that bloody kit with the effort I've given to be here. I'd paid for that with all the international tickets I'd bought over the years when growing up. Don't take it away from me.'

But I didn't. I skulked away. My eyes stared at the floor. It was like seeing the Christmas present you'd always longed for there in front of you and then being taken away at the last minute. 'Spikey's' words rung out in my head, "Go training, fake an injury and get your kit...get your kit." Why hadn't I listened to him?

'Spikey' went on to lead Wales B to a famous win on French soil. The entire B squad returned to Wales as heroes and gave the selectors something to think about. I locked myself away in my house.

In the February I got engaged. I remember the day well because it was the same day 'Spikey' captained Wales to a brilliant victory in Dublin against the Irish. After the B match in November there had been a huge outcry for my captain at

Newport to take charge of the national side. We were over in Liz's cousin's house having a bit of a party. Everyone was congratulating us on our engagement. I was trying to be polite while my eyes were glued to the TV screen.

I didn't want to watch Wales play, but I did. I know that sounds stupid. It was great to see Wales win and 'Spikey' leading the troops so well, but my mind couldn't help thinking that it could have been me out in Dublin playing full-back. Howell Davies, who had played in that B international against France, won his second Welsh cap that day.

Howell was a fine full-back and an excellent goal kicker who fully deserved to play, but I really thought, 'It could have been me'. I'm not saying that I would have definitely got into the side, there are always a lot of 'ifs' and 'buts' in these circumstances, but I was almost there – within touching distance from the prize I'd always dreamt about. The dream I had when I would play on the tump of grass near my house in Ely. Life, as they say, is all about fine margins.

My groin continued to cause me problems. I was told to rest as much as possible but as a sports teacher and also a bit of a fitness fanatic it was hard. Telling a fitness fanatic to take it easy is like telling an alcoholic to give up drinking while he's working in a pub. My brain couldn't cope with the injury and with the chemical changes occurring in my body. Going from being fit and training every day, to not training played havoc with me. Training had been my drug of choice – a drug I needed but a drug all the same – and I found it very hard to wean myself off it. I needed that hit of endorphins.

My injury wasn't getting any better and I started to think for the first time my career may be over – over before it had really begun – washed up on the beach of despair at the ripe old age of 22. It was hard to take. I needed to look for a chink of light at the end of this tunnel.

IN A 'NEWPORT STATE OF MIND'

One of the greatest and nicest men I have ever met in rugby was Dr. Lindsay Robling. He was the team doctor at Newport. After examining me he sent me to the Royal Gwent Hospital for an X-ray. They did lots of tests, like making me stand on one leg like a ballerina, and all kinds of weird stuff before the diagnosis was finally given – I had inflammation of the pelvic bone. At last, I now had a reason for the niggling injury that had prevented me being part of the Wales B squad.

It was a condition called Osteitis Pubis Symphysis – quite a rare condition, particularly in rugby players. Apparently one of the causes can be from overtraining. Lindsay then suggested I go to the Hillingdon Hospital in Middlesex to see Peter Sperryn, a doctor to the British Olympic team.

On arrival at Hillingdon, I was suprised to be rushed, almost immediately, through to see Dr. Sperryn – a small guy in thick glasses – who seemed more than pleased to see me. It turned out he was fascinated by my condition. He was writing a research paper on the injury and, because of its rarity in rugby players, I guess I became a bit of a guinea pig for him. He took personal care of me which was quite a privilege.

He discovered that one side of my pelvis was shorter than the other, causing an imbalance in my movement which was resulting in the pubic joint becoming inflamed. I was told it was a condition not uncommon in women during pregnancy but, naturally, I kept that part quiet when explaining the injury to my team mates! He recommended I wear a built-up shoe on my left foot, so I sent all my footwear away to be altered. Amazingly, he was spot-on as wearing the built-up shoes and rugby boots – and having lots of rest – really did the trick.

That April, I had my first taste of physical activity for nearly six months – a bike ride. It was only about six miles but it was tough, painful and lung-bursting. However, that feeling of exhaustion made me strangely elated as I knew that I'd taken the first step on the long road back to fitness and to playing again. I'm sure many sportsmen and women would recognise that emotion.

With my built-up boot working wonders, by the summer of 1984 I was fighting fit. Pre-season training soon came around and I was back with the boys doing what I loved, albeit at the expense of gaining the new nickname of 'Club Foot'!

At the end of the previous season, Newport hadn't been playing that well, despite the fact that the forwards were still a match for anyone, but overall the team struggled to turn possession into points. It was good to hear people saying they couldn't wait for my return.

I learnt the hard way that if a player is out of a team – if he's injured, dropped or on the bench – it doesn't matter how much you love your team, deep down a part of you wants that team to do badly and what's more, you hope the player playing in your position has a stinker in every match. Is that human nature? I don't know. I believe that players – when they're not playing – who say they want their team to win, are being economical with the truth. No one will admit it. Even at international level.

I was no different. I wanted players and fans and the management to be saying 'If only Steeley had been playing, perhaps we'd have won.' It's one of the worst feelings in the world to walk into that changing room when your team has won well and, worse still, the player in your position has had a stormer. The last place I wanted to be was in there, but I knew it had to be done. I would put on a brave and false face, pat everyone on the back and tell them how good they all were. I didn't want to go in and certainly didn't feel part of it. I hated it. They were all there in their kit, laughing and joking, while I stood in my civvies with a false smile on my face.

Thankfully, that was all behind me now. I was back playing and going to make the most of it.

In the summer, I'd been training well and had got back to fitness, my confidence restored. I got straight back into the team and scored a try against Coventry in the season opener at Rodney Parade. I was back amongst the boys in the changing rooms. I was one of the gang again.

The following Saturday, against Bristol at home, I tackled Bob Hesford, the England number eight. He went down like he'd been shot. I could hear the crowd, oooo'ing and arrring and clapping. The next thing I remember it was half-time and I was holding an orange on the halfway line. I'd apparently knocked myself out in the tackle and didn't know where the hell I was. Concussed, I was taken away by the doctor.

Once more I was out for the mandatory three weeks. It seemed every time I took one step forward I'd be forced to take another three steps back. A young lad named Jonathan Callard, a superb player who later went on to play for England, got drafted into my position. To be honest, he did very well.

Inside me, the demons started to awaken. The doubts came alive, nagging at me, poking me with a stick. I tried to cast them to the back of my mind and carry on. It wasn't easy.

It took me a few weeks to get back into the side. Again, I was playing reasonably well until that fateful day against Glamorgan Wanderers when I damaged my knee ligaments and my life came tumbling down.

Outside the world of rugby, my life – before that injury and subsequent breakdown – had been going well. I'd got engaged to Liz, we were having a house built and it was great to see it taking shape. We were busy planning our wedding and although I got a bit down I was frustrated, not despondent and far from being depressed.

After my knee ligaments injury, the depression knocked me

to the ground with a hell of a punch. The demons inside me came alive and were having a 24/7 non-stop party. They moved in and refused to leave.

From October 1984 to February 1985, I had four and a half months of pure hell. It got so bad I couldn't sleep – I became anxious by the slightest of things – and I started to cry a lot. Every time Liz went out I'd phone her house, just to make sure she'd got home safely. Stupid, irrational thoughts popped into my head. I understand that people who suffer from schizophrenia hear voices in their heads. I didn't have voices but I had distorted thoughts, terrible thoughts about something bad happening to Liz or my parents. There was no rhyme or reason for it, just things spinning constantly around my head.

At school, I put on a brave face and tried to keep everything together – I had to, it was my job. I'd been on sick leave for six weeks anyway with the injury so I needed to be professional about it. I'm not ashamed to say that I cried every morning before going to school. The irony of a teacher, not a pupil, crying about going to school was not lost on me. It got to the stage where I would simply wade through the day until it was time to go home. It was so unlike me. Only months earlier, I just couldn't wait to get to school to teach the kids – watch them shine as they played sport – and even help them to learn some Cardiff French! Now, I didn't have the emotional space in my mind to care. I slowly became a shadow of my former self. All the joy was being sucked out of me. I cried between lessons. I'd shut the door of my office and sob and sob until I was empty.

I slowly changed from being a colourful character to being a grey lifeless shell. I must have looked terrible. My life became black with small bits of grey here and there – nothing gave any pleasure. I couldn't sit down and watch TV. I couldn't read a book or listen to music anymore. I was anxious all of the time. My nerves seemed to be out of control. My insides felt as though they were bouncing up and down on a big trampoline.

The anxiety came over me in waves. When I got back from work I'd rush upstairs and burst out crying before reaching the top step. The release made it feel better for a while but it was short lived.

My thoughts became distorted and so random. If I heard a song on the radio which had been a hit before me and Liz got together, I'd think 'I bet her and her last boyfriend listened to it.' I'd start to wonder what they'd have been doing at that time. It was so stupid. I didn't know why I was suddenly putting myself through this misery. I loved her and she loved me.

Then in a bizarre twist, I was watching a play on TV about a man having a secret affair and I started worrying that I would have an affair. Not Liz, me! From out of nowhere the thought raced around my head. I didn't know why – I didn't even want an affair – I was in the best relationship in the world so why the hell would I want to jeopardize all that for a fling with someone I hadn't met. It was senseless. It was just my mind playing tricks with me. It felt as though something inside of me was trying its best to screw me up. Some evil demon, mischievously trying its best to drive me insane!

The crazy thing was, I probably worried more about just thinking I was going to have an affair than those people who really were having affairs were worried about being caught.

How bizarre to witness my normal self having arguments and pitched battles against those disturbed thoughts.

On one occasion, as I sat in church one Sunday, my mind started to wander – as it normally did. From deep inside my mind, the most bizarre question just popped out. 'What would it be like to be a priest?' popped into it.

'What?' I almost answered back, aloud.

'Being a priest. I bet it would be a cosy number, a few services a week, nice house, food given to you. Why don't you become a priest? Come on! You'd be good at it.'

'I don't want to be a bloody priest. I'm getting married.'

'Be a priest'

'No I'm getting married.'

'Priest.'

'No!'

'Yes!'

'No!'

This went on for the rest of the service and beyond. Day after day I'd have this battle and it almost felt as if I'd been possessed. I half expected someone to tie me to my bed and throw holy water on me as I spewed green gunk over them, whilst talking in strange tongues. It's very odd thinking about it now but, at the time, it was terrifying.

If I was at school and I'd given a kid a row for doing something wrong it would worry me. If he cried I'd be overcome with guilt and think, 'You're going to get the sack now. His mother's going to come down the school and complain to the headmaster and that will be it. You've gone too far.'

My mind would question everything I did, in a negative way. No matter what I was doing my mind was telling me it was not good enough, useless or bad.

Imagine having that pressure going on in your head all day, every day. On top of that, I couldn't sleep. I hadn't slept properly for weeks. It was clearly a recipe for disaster. I had no peace of mind – no comfort in relaxation. My mind was more like a war-zone with bullets and bombs flying about all over the place. It would never switch off. It was a exhausting place to be.

Liz began to learn to spot the danger signs that things weren't going well for me.

She would ask, "Are you ok?"

"No I'm struggling. How do you know?"

"Because you've gone quiet. You've disengaged from the world."

To the outside world I looked alright I guess. But inside, there were constant battles going on. Like a bunch of mad, nasty, cartoon characters running amok in my brain.

Certain thoughts would leap into my mind and torment me for about four or five days. Then my mind would get 'bored' by it. However that didn't mean respite, on the contrary, it was merely the trigger for another unwanted, illogical thought to take its turn to distress me.

On occasions, I just wanted to run somewhere but I didn't know where and even if I'd got somewhere I knew running from it wouldn't be right. Shouting and screaming didn't help either. The only thing that eased it for a while was crying – it was my only release valve. It made me feel better for a while, engaging my mind in an uneasy truce before it started up again.

My teaching colleagues at the school noticed the change in me. They could tell something wasn't right and tried to help me but I didn't realise what was happening. I was a man, and men didn't get depression. I thought it was just a phase – I was just being miserable not depressed. I had no idea because I was in a maelstrom. It was a lot harder as well in those days. There wasn't Google or the internet to research my symptoms. To be honest, at times I was so bad I couldn't have sat by a computer for more than two minutes even if it had been available.

Talking about it to others at that time was definitely a taboo subject – a no-go area. I was still functioning, or thinking I was functioning properly, but I could have been a wreck – I simply couldn't tell. Inside there were questions and doubts and fears. My confidence simply eroded away. I started to think people were talking about me, and not in a good way, which compounded my anxiety. It was definitely not a good place to be.

Then things got darker, a lot darker. I had my first suicidal thought in early 1985, when I was doing a spot of coaching with my local club, Caerau Ely. Since I wasn't playing due to the knee injury, they asked if I would take a few training sessions for them. I agreed. I needed to do something to stop me from losing the plot. One night, while the players were all running around the pitch doing some warm-ups, I stood in the middle – just watching – when out of nowhere I had the scariest of thoughts.

'There's no point in all this, is there?' The words filled my head, 'what's the point in going on? Wouldn't you and everyone else be better off if you weren't here anymore? Isn't it time to...you know...just end it.'

The shocking thing was it wasn't a shock. It seemed the most natural thing to do. To make matters worse, the words spinning around my head sounded more sinister than the ones before. My depression knew it was planting the 'suicide seed' in my mind. I heard it as a deep voice – an older, all-encompassing voice – whispering in my head. While the other thoughts I'd had, like being a priest and having an affair, were stupid and seemed illogical to me, this one didn't. It was rational. It had a peaceful serenity about it.

Whilst the other thoughts appeared to be very confrontational – as if they wanted a reaction, a battle – when it came to the suicidal one, it seemed to be sympathetic and reassuring. It wasn't looking for a battle. It was as if my depression was trying to help me do the obvious and reasonable thing. It was a horrible feeling and although I knew it was wrong and I didn't want to do it, my mind didn't want to battle against it.

As the boys were still running around the field, I seemed to just accept what my thoughts were telling me to do. That's how scary it had become. I now understand, from my research into depression and from speaking to other sufferers, that people who commit suicide, or attempt to do so, have come to believe that it is the only viable option left open to them.

A few minutes later when the players had reached me, I'd sidelined my dark thought and switched back into coaching mode.

"Okay" I said, "Let's have a game of touch rugby." I needed to do something to be involved in the action. Something to take my mind off, well, my mind!

Sadly, the suicidal thought hadn't completely disappeared. It still lurked in the shadows of my mind. It would leap out now and again and whisper in that calm voice, especially when my mind had got to a very low place. The thoughts lasted a few minutes then they hid away again.

Perhaps many people, more than we all realise, have similar dark thoughts. With some it probably comes and then goes in a flash, as part of the 'normal' thinking process, but with others – including me – it just clung on like a limpet and you can't separate yourself from it. My depression was like a skilful cowboy hanging on to a bucking horse at a rodeo. No matter how hard I fought, it was always there, waiting for the next opportunity.

Although I told people about some of the things going on in my head, I never mentioned that one. Maybe I was ashamed, embarrassed, or a mixture of both. Looking back now I really believe I was so lucky to have been doing things to keep my mind active and to prevent those thoughts from coming back. I really can't begin to imagine what may have happened if I'd been living alone, with no family, or girlfriend or friends around me. Even writing this now, I physically shiver at the thought of what I could have done.

During my darkest time I'd gone to see the local GP to tell him about it. He prescribed some pills. I didn't think pills would help. I thought the problem was in my brain, not my body but what I didn't understand then, and what he tried to explain, was that the human body consists of a mixture of different chemicals – we're essentially (in simple terms) a concoction of chemicals within a soul – and when that mixture becomes imbalanced we become ill, whether it be cancer, diabetes or depression.

"Depression," he said, "is just an imbalance of the chemicals in your brain."

Today I can see the logic in that, but back then I just couldn't comprehend it. Ignorance is a terrible thing. In those days I couldn't get my head around how a pill could stop me thinking horrible distressing thoughts.

My mother, a strict Catholic, was very 'old school' about the whole thing. "You don't need pills," she told me, "you are a qualified teacher, and you play full-back for Newport. You aren't some poor bloke who can't cope with life. You are strong and brave. You're a somebody."

Don't ask me why but, in a moment of weakness, I flushed all of the tablets down the toilet. It was the worst mistake I've ever made in my life. I wish I hadn't because maybe my life would have been different. I simply wasn't mature enough, and without the wisdom or desire to understand. Also, there was a stigma about people suffering from depression. They were all bonkers and people who had to take tablets for being bonkers were even more bonkers.

When I look back now it is astonishing to think I was still able to continue with what must have seemed a 'normal' life to onlookers; still going to work and carrying out the mundane day to day tasks of life. That is the most insidious thing about depression – it has very few outward signs. You're not in a wheelchair, in plaster or on crutches which might at least gain you a degree of sympathy from others. On the contrary, with depression the pain is internalised and as it makes a sufferer sad, miserable, irritable and not good company. It often invites scorn rather than sympathy.

It must have been a terrible time for Liz and my family. Inevitably loved ones bear the brunt of helping and caring for someone with depression. The patience, understanding and selflessness shown to me by my mum and dad and especially by Liz, was unbelievable. She could have quite understandably walked away from our relationship but she didn't. In fact the worse I became, the more she showed her love for me.

The other pernicious thing about depression is that even when a person starts to recover, the improvement is rarely straightforward – there is no such thing as a straight line recovery – and this can be extremely frustrating. Indeed it takes a huge effort to avoid being sucked into a downward spiral all over again.

However, over the following months I gradually got better. With a wedding to organise I kept my brain active with normal and happy thoughts, which prevented the depression – still lurking in the background – having any opportunity to dominate my thoughts. The dark clouds dispersed but although I was much improved, I definitely wasn't the same bloke I had been before the injury.

I didn't realise at the time how it would affect me for years to come. It left me with a dreadful, chronic anxiety which was like living life under a cloak of constant unease.

5

Marriage, Birth and Deaths

'I found traditional learning very difficult and Mr. Steele, as he was known to me then, gave me a release from the classroom by introducing me to a rugby ball, knowing that I was at my happiest out on the pitch. That was the start of my sporting journey and I owe Phil a lot for the time and effort, on and off the field, and for the great support and advice he gave me and my family. Who would have predicted all those years ago that I, as a chubby number eight, would manage to become a better full-back than him!'

Lee Byrne –Wales and British & Irish Lions

My stag night took place at the Wenvoe Arms on a Thursday night, a week before the start of the school summer holidays. Stag nights in those days didn't see gangs of men getting dressed up like superheroes and jetting off to Spain for the weekend. This was a proper, old fashioned stag do. It consisted of us all sitting in the same pub all night, drinking plenty of beer, singing and drinking more beer with lots of laughter in between. Not surprisingly I didn't make it in to school until mid-day the following day. I was in no fit state to go. I should have really stayed home, but I had to show my face because it happened to be our school's sports day. I knew it wouldn't look good for the PE teacher to miss it, stag night or no stag night.

With my head banging like a drum, and looking worse for wear I staggered into school to be greeted with great cheers from teachers and pupils alike. I seemed to be a bigger hero for making it in at midday than if I had been there at 7.30am, marking out the running track. All the other teachers took great pleasure in taking the mickey out of me – although some of them were in just as bad a state as I was. Those were the days of teaching when rightly or wrongly, it was acceptable to go out and have a few with your colleagues after work. It was part of the bonding process.

The following day – Friday, 19 July 1985 – was quite a poignant day in my life. Not only was it the last day of the school summer term, it was also the last day before I changed schools, and the last day of my life as a single man.

Liz and I were married in my home parish church of St. Francis in Ely, even though Liz wasn't a Catholic. Liz and her mother were very gracious in agreeing to this as it was tradition that the choice of church was usually the bride's. Needless to say, my mother was as pleased as punch.

The wedding day itself was fantastic. It was an amalgamation of being like a star on 'This Is Your Life' and the Queen at the FA Cup Final, with all our relatives and friends in one place and all those hands to shake!

My best man was my great college friend Ithel Davies from the village of Gwaun Cae Gurwen in the Amman Valley, the same village as Gareth Edwards. Ithel had that priceless gift of being rib-ticklingly funny without even meaning to be. I loved his dry humour and his quirky sayings which he delivered with a deadpan expression and a sprinkling of Welsh. I've never forgotten the opening line of his speech:

"When Phil first asked me to be his best man, I first of all thought to myself, 'That's a great honour, I don't really deserve that.' Then I thought, 'there again, I've got Athlete's foot and I don't really deserve that either.'"

It was such a simple line but delivered by Ithel it brought the house down. I still often use a similar version to begin my after-dinner speeches today.

After the wedding, Liz and I jetted off on honeymoon to Guernsey. Well, I say jetted, it was actually a four-hour drive to Weymouth in my clapped-out Ford Fiesta, followed by five hours on the ferry to the Channel Islands.

The funny thing was, I packed my running spikes and rugby ball so I could also squeeze in a bit of training. It's ok, Liz knew I had them with me – I hadn't sneaked them in the car without her knowing. Hence, in between doing things couples do on their honeymoon, I took Liz to a nearby playing field and had her kicking the ball to me.

"Can we go back to the hotel now?" she asked after her 100th high ball. "I'm tired and my feet hurt."

"Let's do a few dozen grubber kicks first, love."

Who says romance is dead? Back then I knew how to show a girl a good time. God only knows what she thought. Luckily we were married by then and it was too late to kick me into touch. Not the most amorous way to spend your honeymoon. But that was me.

I often ponder that scenario today when I hear people say how dedicated and single-minded the top modern professional rugby players need to be in order to reach the pinnacle, and indeed I bow to no man in my admiration for them in doing what it takes to succeed at the very top.

Yet in our own way, players in the amateur era had to be just as committed and dedicated, whether it be fitting in a sprint session during the school lunch hour, or taking part in as many as three cross-country runs a day with the kids or doing some goal kicking practice on a Sunday morning with my new wife on our honeymoon. We had to take every opportunity to keep ourselves fit to play rugby whilst coping with a full-time job.

On our way back to Wales, we were stopped by the customs official who decided to search the car from top to bottom. We had no idea what he thought he would find.

"What's the occasion?" he asked.

"It's our honeymoon," I replied.

"What's in there?" he said, pointing to a bag in the boot.

"It's only my spikes and a rugby ball."

'There's the Welsh for you – rugby mad,' he must have been thinking by the look of the strange glance he gave us as he waved us through.

On our return to Wales we settled down in a small two-bedroomed house in Taff's Well. The main reason we ended up there was it was far cheaper than buying a property in Cardiff itself. Even so, it still seemed far removed from Ely. We Cardiffians joked that anywhere past the Monaco Cinema in Rhiwbina was classed as 'North Wales' and anywhere beyond the Red Lion pub in Bonvilston was deemed 'West Wales'.

So, with me from Ely and Liz being from St. Mellons, we moved over the invisible border and became 'valley' folk. The first thing I noticed was how different the accent was and how the pace of life seemed a lot more relaxed even though we were less than two miles from the outskirts of the city. There was nothing wrong with that, nothing at all, it was just a little bit of a culture shock for a Cardiff lad.

In the September I started teaching at St. Michael's RC Primary School in Treforest. Again, my main focus was teaching PE but I also had to take the odd class or two in the delights of Religious Education. I wasn't sure if I was knowledgeable enough in the workings of the church to teach kids all about guilt and salvation in four easy stages, but I gave it a go anyway. It was quite an eye opener for me as well as them!

In Catholic education the clergy were regarded as god-like characters and the parish priest automatically sat as chairman of the governors.

When I had the interview for the job, the headmaster asked me: "How in an athletics lesson would you teach baton changing to a class of eight-year-olds?" It was sports related so I went into great detail on how it should be done.

Then the priest, with a stare that would have frozen hell over, leant in and muttered, "What do you think should happen if a teacher is found to be having an extra-marital affair?"

I sat there for a minute, silently trying to figure out the relevance of the question to the job I was being interviewed for. Was he testing my morals? Maybe he didn't know anything about sport and had been reading Marjorie Proops' problem page that morning while eating his toast.

I really didn't understand how answering that question would help me teach a kid to spin-pass a rugby ball or do a back-flip. 'Well done Michael ... your tackling is very good. Your head and body position are at just the right angle but don't forget, don't ever have an extra-marital affair, or you will never go on to play for Wales.'

I can't remember what reply I came back with but it must have worked because they offered me the job.

During my time at St. Michael's I crossed paths with the headmaster too many times to remember. Con McCarthy was a tall, domineering man who scared everyone with his booming voice and stern demeanour, and that was just the staff!

He was a good man and devout Catholic but his philosophy of primary school sport was poles apart from mine. He wanted excellence for the school and trophies in the cabinet. His mentality towards sport was to 'win at all costs'. Don't forget this was a school of Under-11s, not the New Zealand All Blacks.

Our opposing philosophies led to numerous clashes between us, behind the closed door of his office. My aim was a lot simpler than his. Of course I wanted the kids to win matches and be successful but, more importantly, I wanted them to enjoy it. I wanted to be able to send all my 30 kids to the comprehensive school at the age of 11 with a love of sport and physical activity. I didn't care if it was rugby, or soccer, or running or whatever, as long as they tried it and liked it. Did it really matter if they were any good at it? If it excited them and they got involved, I had done my job. We won games on the way, which was a bonus, but that was never the over-riding priority in my eyes.

The headmaster didn't see it that way. He'd stress the need to beat our opponents at the weekend and ask me how we were going to do it.

I remember we lost to the local Welsh language school, Ysgol Pont Siôn Norton, in a cup match one Saturday morning. The following Monday I sat in class and over the tannoy I heard the announcement: "Mr. Steele. Can you please come to my office?"

There was no, 'Good morning everyone' or 'What a lovely day it is today' so, as I walked to his office, I had a feeling this wasn't going to be a 'pay rise and a pat on the back' type of meeting. After knocking his door and walking in, I could see by the expression on his face that he wasn't a happy man. I sat bolt upright in the chair as he dispensed with any pleasantries and got right to the point.

"How the hell did we lose a cup match to them? ... The first time in our history ... Why did we pick boy X and not boy Y?"

I was lost for words. We had lost in an Under-11s cup match. It wasn't the Welsh international team failing to get out of their group at the Rugby World Cup! The boys from Ysgol Pont Siôn

Norton had won because they deserved to – 'fair play', or in their case *'chwarae teg'*. That is what sport is all about.

I was young and fiery back then and I wouldn't just back down. I had recently graduated from the best PE training college in Britain and I wasn't going to let a man, who had probably never picked up a rugby ball in his life, dictate to me. I had a set phrase which I always pulled out of my locker at times like these. "Well, Mr. McCarthy, I have a degree in physical education from South Glamorgan Institute, the best there is, and that's why you employed me. So I think that qualifies me to decide which of the two 10-year-old boys is more suited to playing at scrum-half don't you?"

I walked out, leaving him speechless. I used that retort many times over the next few years, changing the odd word here and there.

I recall one time when a new boy arrived at the school. Together with his mother and sister, they had been relocated to Pontypridd from Glasgow because of domestic violence in the family. Apparently the father had physically attacked them, so they'd come to Pontypridd to stay at a refuge for victims of domestic violence.

"Mr. Steele," the headmaster said, "I'm starting the new boy in your class."

To be honest, the little fella was a nervous wreck and almost on the verge of tipping over. He was so traumatised he'd cry during lessons and wouldn't speak – what is now called a 'selective mute' – the poor kid. However I did my best to encourage him and to bring him out of his shell. Slowly he turned a corner and showed me and everyone else what a great kid he was. He eventually came on school trips and got involved in sport. Rugby helped to bring him out of himself.

He'd only been there for a few days when the headmaster stopped me in the corridor, "How's the new lad, Mr. Steele?"

"He's in a bit of a state ... it will take time."

"Have you tested him yet?"

"Yes. I've done a reading test, an English test, a Maths test ..."

"No!" he almost yelled, "have you tested him over a hundred metres yet? He may have a bit of pace. We could do with a good winger."

I walked away, shaking my head in disbelief.

On another occasion, his voice over the tannoy once again summoned me to his office. We hadn't recently lost a game so I wearily headed along the corridor thinking, 'What now ... I can't take much more of this.' However to my great surprise, sitting there in the headmaster's office, was the Ireland and British Lions prop Gerry McLaughlin. He had moved to Wales and opened a wine bar in Gilfach Goch. Being a 'good Catholic boy', he'd brought his kids to our school. With cup final victories flashing before our headmaster's eyes, he asked our guest if he fancied helping out with the team. Normally I would have gone crazy if the headmaster had asked someone to help me out but, on this occasion, I didn't mind as it was great to work alongside the British Lion prop, who'd kindly agreed to coach our forward pack.

For all the headmaster's faults, as I saw them, I did eventually grow to respect him and I'd like to think that the feeling was mutual. He was unbelievably committed to the school and under him the children enjoyed an outstanding education – we were classed as a high-performing school. It was a different era to today as far as sport was concerned. In those days we played every Saturday morning and trained a few nights a week as well. There was lots of competition between schools and even the occasional bout of snobbery.

Once we were invited to take the school team to compete in a 7s tournament at Edgarley Hall, the preparatory school for the famous Millfield School in Somerset which counted Gareth Edwards and JPR Williams among its alumni.

During the afternoon I got invited to the headmaster's tent for a glass of rum punch. Yes, I know, a world away from Pontypridd refreshments. A smartly dressed lady with a pristine, cut glass English accent walked up to me and said. "And which school are you?"

"St. Michael's in Treforest." I replied.

"I don't know the name, where exactly is this Treforest?"

"It's about a mile further up from Rhydyfelin!" I responded mischievously.

"Oh yes ... I see ... you're from the state sector." She quickly turned tail and scurried off.

I had the last laugh though. Although we didn't win the tournament, my boys conducted themselves perfectly both on and off the pitch. I was so proud of them. I used to insist that every one of my kids shook hands with the referee – win, lose or draw – after the game. I wanted them to grow up respecting authority. Maybe it was my mother's influence, harking back to the occasions she made us shake hands with our Uncle Michael. Subconsciously, the ref could have been my Uncle Michael.

Even though the teaching hours were long, I didn't mind one bit and I was often at the school longer than I should have been. When my daughter Bryony was very young, Liz would bring her to the school in her pushchair – where I'd be busy out on the field, marking out the running track or something similar – just so I could see her before she went to bed.

Today the kids in primary school may not even have a male teacher to take them for sport. I'm not for one minute saying that women teachers cannot do the same – or a better – job than men, but there's a definite need for there to be more male role models in the teaching profession at primary level. There must be an equal mix.

MARRIAGE, BIRTH AND DEATHS

Liz and I had been married for three months when, in October 1985, my mother Nancy – who by then was 63 – started complaining about a bad back. Even at our wedding, the previous July, she had been in pain but now it was getting much worse.

One evening my father got us four kids together and told us it wasn't looking very good for our mother. She'd been to hospital for tests and the doctor had told her she had bone cancer, and it was terminal.

The words bone cancer and terminal are not words you want to hear about anyone, especially a close family member. As far as deaths in our family, we had been lucky up to that point as only my gran had died. She was old and it was natural causes so we had been ready and prepared for that, but my mother was still relatively young. She was still larger than life itself, still hardworking and still as bright as a button.

He didn't say how long she had but added, "You know your mother will worry about you, so I don't want you to let her know that you know she is dying because then she will worry about how we'll all cope without her, and that will upset her even more. I want you all to act as normal."

Act as normal? How could I act as normal after hearing news like that? I understood my father's wishes, and that he thought he was doing his best for my mother, but it was so hard for all of us. It was as if a screen had unexpectedly been put up between us. It felt akin to my mother being put in prison and talking to us from behind a sheet of glass. An invisible barrier had been erected overnight.

When we talked, I couldn't be open with her, and doubtless she couldn't be the same with me. It felt a bit like a conversation between two people when one of them has to say something important, yet something they know the other person won't like, so they decide against it and resort to small talk. That's how it felt for our family. From that day on, whenever we were with my mother, it was a life of small talk. I really wanted us to cut to the chase and savour every last moment with her. To tear down that invisible screen and *cwtch* her and tell her that I knew she was dying but that I loved her and we were all ok. Thinking of it now it was heart-breaking. I'm still not sure if it had been the right or wrong thing to do. I've always wondered if it was the same for her. That's the big question I've asked myself every day since.

By the middle of December things deteriorated so rapidly she was confined to her bed. I'd go and see her and try and be normal. "Never mind Mum," I said, trying to comfort her. In the New Year you'll be able to come and see me play rugby and then the cricket in the summer."

She'd nod but I could tell by her eyes, she knew she wouldn't be there. When I left I would be sobbing so much I'd have to stop the car. The last time I saw her alive was 23 December 1985.

As I left I said, "I love you Mum."

I don't remember ever saying that to her before. We weren't that type of family. We loved each other but we never spoke to each other in that way.

On Christmas Eve she went into a coma and the parish priest, Father Henneberry, gave her the Last Rites. We all stood around the bed, heartbroken. He prayed, "On this special feast of Christmas, we ask you, God, to take Nancy to a better place."

I thought, 'Oh ... of course ... it's Christmas.' Even though we'd decorated the house, the whole thing had passed me by. It was our first Christmas as a married couple but I couldn't have felt less like enjoying the festivities. She passed away five minutes after midnight on Christmas Day.

It was the most un-Christmas, Christmas Day ever. The first three people I spoke to were – in order – my father, a MacMillan nurse who came to lay my mother out, and Mr. Pidgeon the funeral director.

My mother was the first person really close to me to pass away. It had a big effect on me to think she wouldn't be there anymore for us. It made me start to think of Christianity in a different light. Growing up I became an automatic Catholic – I didn't have a choice in it – but my mother's death made me start to rethink about life, spirituality and faith. My faith became stronger but it wasn't necessarily just a Catholic faith anymore. I came round to thinking that something bigger existed, but I wasn't sure what.

As far as my depression was concerned I didn't feel any worse than I had before my mother's death. I still had anxiety and and, naturally, the whole event made me very unsettled but I kept it all together, which surprised me.

Rugby wise I decided to go back to Glamorgan Wanderers. My head wasn't in the game at Newport and I couldn't keep a regular place in the team. I'd lost interest and my confidence had deteriorated at the same time, so going back to Glamorgan Wanderers was my way of wrapping myself up in my little comfort blanket once again.

On a much more positive note, Liz fell pregnant right at the end of 1986 and, on 14 August 1987, Bryony was born. That was another life-changing experience. I can tell you now, there was plenty of gas and air consumed that day – Liz had some as well. There I was, all suited up in gown and mask – in cricket parlance, at the non-striker's end – waiting for the delivery to arrive!!

Bryony was the most beautiful thing I'd ever seen. I know all fathers say that, but in my eyes she was and still is.

Holding her in my arms brought back memories of my mum and how she would have loved meeting her granddaughter. She would have wrapped her up in her arms and probably rushed her off to the nearest church to get her baptised. In the olden days, the Catholic tradition was that the first time the parents took a baby out of the house it should only be to get the child baptised. "Because if something happened to the baby before they were baptised," my mother told us, "they would not be allowed into heaven and they will be forever floating about in limbo."

Now how frightening must that have been to young parents with new babies? To be honest whoever came up with that one must have been some kind of marketing genius. Scaring people into quickly committing their children to the cause, for fear they'd go to purgatory. Brilliant!

Having a baby is a stressful time. I didn't realise just how much until Bryony came along. Everything is a worry but, in my opinion, whoever invented the children's medicine Calpol is up there in the Pantheon with Pasteur, Marie Curie, Fleming and all the other medical greats! On the odd occasion when Bryony fell ill, the first thing that popped into my mind was ringing my mother. I wanted to hear her voice. I wanted her to tell me there was nothing wrong and it was all normal. I wanted the comfort from her that only mothers could give. Again it was at those times that her loss hit me hard.

By the middle of July 1988, I'd got sick and tired of arguing with the headmaster at St. Michael's. I realised that I needed to move on, so I applied for the post of PE teacher at St. Mary's RC Primary School in Bridgend.

At the time of the job interview Liz and I were moving house and, being at the height of a property boom, the whole process was going through very quickly. Like all people buying and selling houses, we were receiving lots of letters from estate agents and solicitors concerning the guy buying our house, a Mr. Price. His name has been spinning around my head for weeks and it almost cost me a job.

At St. Mary's I was welcomed by the headmaster, a Mr. Lloyd, who introduced me to a row of priests. It was like a scene from *Father Ted*. As with my previous interview at St. Michael's the priests seemed more interested in how I would save the world from evil than how I could teach the children about sport.

I was ready this time. "Sport can help the children learn about fair play, teamwork, sportsmanship and tolerance." I reeled off a long list of Christian qualities that I felt could be developed through playing sport. I think I almost referred back to *The Simple Prayer Book* and said that sport could prevent one from 'Coveting his neighbour's ass' or 'committing adultery!' I was more relaxed by now and turned to one of the priests after being asked a question and started my answer by saying: "As I was saying to Mr. Price earlier..."

All the way through the hour long interrogation I kept calling the head, Mr Price.

On leaving, the headmaster walked me to my car. "Well done Mr. Steele. Congratulations, you've got the job. I look forward to seeing see you in September."

Shaking his hand, I added, "Thank you Mr. Price, that's great news."

He stopped me in my tracks. "By the way, my name is Lloyd," he said.

Then, puffing out my chest and endeavouring to look and sound like a consummate professional – after assuming my new boss had given me permission to address him by his first name – I turned and said: "Thank you Mr. Price and that's very kind of you but, if you don't mind, I'll call you Lloyd out of school and Mr. Price when we're at work. If that's okay with you?"

"No Mr. Steele. Lloyd is my surname!" he replied, smiling.

The poor man must have felt like he was starring in some

comedy sketch. I bid him a hasty goodbye and laughed with embarrassment all the way back to Taff's Well.

It was at St. Mary's that I first came across a young lad who was about nine at the time. He wasn't the most confident in the classroom and needed extra help with his reading but put him on the games field and he came alive! He was skilful, intelligent and dominant. I saw first-hand how PE and sport could be a massive confidence developer in less academic pupils.

He played in the back row of the school team and I remember thinking that if this lad develops he could be a very useful player. His name was Lee Byrne and he eventually went on to play full-back for Wales and the Lions.

One of the most exciting days I've ever had as a commentator was at the Millennium Stadium in November 2005 when Wales were playing the All Blacks. As a freelancer, I was reporting on the radio for RTÉ (the Irish state broadcaster) because Ireland were to play the All Blacks the following week.

Around 15 minutes from full-time, with Wales losing heavily, the radio station came to me for an update. I was all prepared to start what I thought would be an insightful and in-depth description of how good the All Blacks had been, and what Ireland would need to do the following week to have a chance against them. However, as the presenter was about to cue over to me, I looked at my scoresheet and stopwatch: the two most important facts in an update are the score and match time, which are always given first. As I did, I heard a booming voice over the tannoy, announcing: "Replacement for Wales. Number fifteen, Gareth Thomas, is replaced by number twenty-two, Lee Byrne!"

It would be fair to say I was mildly excited! Proficiently and professionally I began: "Sixty-eight minutes gone here at the Millennium Stadium and New Zealand lead Wales by twenty eight points to three." Then I lost it completely and, with a mixture of emotion and elation, continued "and I can tell you that Wales have just brought on their second replacement, it's Scarlets' full-back Lee Byrne and he's a former pupil of mine. I was his PE teacher at St. Mary's Roman Catholic Primary School in Bridgend, and he's the first ever former pupil of mine to play for Wales!"

I can't even recall if I mentioned any scores or scorers! I bet listeners the length of Ireland from Dublin to Dundalk and from Cork to Coleraine were thinking 'Jaysus, what the feck is this mad Welshman going on about?'

Thankfully the presenter joined in the conversation, and when I handed back to him he said something along the lines of, what a special moment it must have been for me. I think that my mention of a Roman Catholic school and, with Byrne being an Irish name, the Dublin-based radio station overlooked my exuberant announcement, and my forgetting to provide their listeners with any important information.

It's a real pleasure that today, more than a quarter of a century since he was my school pupil, I get to work alongside Lee as he develops a burgeoning career as a rugby co-commentator for BBC Wales.

When I arrived home after the interview at St. Mary's, I phoned by father to tell him I'd got the job – naturally leaving out the bit about forgetting the headmaster's name. "As long as you're happy son ... as long as your happy." Those were to be the last words he ever spoke to me.

It had been over two years since my mother had passed away and my father was still walking around like a lost soul. He came to watch me play rugby now and again but he had completely changed. He even started going to Mass every Sunday despite not being a Catholic. I didn't ask him why. I assume he derived some comfort from being in the place that meant so much to my mother.

The following day, I was in the school hall practising with the St. Michael's school choir, who were performing at the Pontypridd festival the following week, with me providing accompaniment on the guitar. The school secretary came in, sheepishly, and told me my brother was on the phone. A shiver raced through my body. I just knew something was wrong. No one from my family ever called me at work.

Trying to keep calm, I rushed down to the office. "Hello John." I was afraid to ask the obvious question. "What's the matter?"

"Phil," he replied, "I'm just phoning to tell you that Dad has had an accident. He's been knocked off his bike."

My entire body went cold and I struggled to ask the next question. "Is he ... is he ... alright?"

"We're not sure ... He's got a head injury and is in intensive care at the Heath hospital."

The more John talked, the worse it sounded. Having words like head injury and intensive care in the same sentence didn't paint a pretty picture. I felt a surge of emotion and fear rushing through my body, as if I was a volcano about to erupt. I immediately hurried out of the school for what seemed like the longest drive of my life.

Dad lay in an intensive care bed, a bandage around his head and his eyes shut. Apparently he had been driving his Honda 50cc motor bike near the Tesco roundabout at Culverhouse Cross, when a car had come up the slip road and knocked him off his bike. The force of the collision had thrown him into the air, dislodging his helmet, before he landed on his head. No one was really to blame. It was just one of those stupid accidents that happen all too frequently.

I couldn't believe it was only 16 hours since I'd spoken to him about my new job. It's strange how a tragic event can bond a family together. The Steele clan all gathered in the waiting

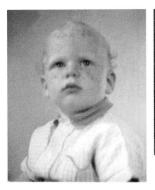

Mum and Dad - Nancy and Jack.

Displaying the typical Phil
Steele hair style – aged
two.

Learning how to pull the birds
with my elder brother John (left)
circa 1963.

Early days as a junior member of
the Ely Mafia!

With my brother John and our next door neighbour, Mrs. Bowen (left). Known as 'Auntie' Ena she was one of the many non-related aunts all Welsh kids have. On the right is our 'real' Auntie Eileen.

At St. Francis junior school circa 1969.

Gavin Henson wasn't the first to have white boots! Me and my brother in Ely.

Commencing studies for the 'A' Level in 'Guilt' as an Altar Boy.

With my three most indispensable items –
cricket bat, rugby boots and guitar!

'Come one Sir!' Clipping one off the legs for Wenvoe CC on tour in the
Potteries, aged 19.

Running the 1981 Cardiff Marathon with journalist
Rob Cole. I had joggers nipple, he didn't!

My last game as a student – for South Glamorgan Institute against Villanova
University in Pennsylvania, USA – in April 1983. Eight of this team went
on to play first class rugby as it used to be known. My great friend, the ex-
Swansea and Wales centre Kevin Hopkins, is back row (far left), with WRU
coaching guru Geraint John back row (fourth from left).

With the lads of Wenvoe CC. The butcher, baker and candlestick maker had nothing on these boys – the most eclectic bunch of men I have come across in any walk of life!

Life is too short not to go on tour. This time to Essex as captain of Cardiff Wanderers Invitation XI in 1991.

PHIL'S FEAST

By DAVID JULIANS

Glam Wanderers 16pts
Neath 13

WANDERERS' full back Phil Steele was the 12-point hero of this victory.

He shook Neath with a try and a penalty in a three-minute spell to give Wanderers a 7—nil half-time lead.

And he laid on a second try for Hugh Davies after Neath had stormed into the lead after the interval. Steele also converted both tries as Wanderers clinched their eighth Merit Table win of the season.

There was no end-of-season look about either side in this thriller.

Neath's two second half tries came in four minutes. Flanker David Morgan scored the first, converted by full back Neale Harris.

Then Welsh youth international Paul Morgan marked his debut with a try after a mistake by hooker Hugh Davies.

Davies got his own back three minutes later when he scored his first try for the club. Steele made a 30-yard break to put him through.

Steele spree sinks Neath

Neath manager Brian Thomas who was in the side who won the WRU Cup 11 years ago, can take heart. The Welsh All-Blacks were nearly over for three first half tries and their attacking display put Wanderers under pressure to the end.

Neath lost Harris, their record points scorer this season, with a leg injury in the 61st minute. Wanderers also had a casualty, Wayne Pritchard retiring with a leg injury in the 29th minute.

Wanderers made life difficult for themselves. Centre Nick Ward missed four penalty kicks in the first 13 minutes before Steele took over.

SCORERS. — Wanderers: Tries, Steele, H. Davies; con. Steele; pens. Steele (2). Neath: Tries, D. Morgan, P. Morgan; con. Harris; pen. I. Davies.

Mighty kick by Steele

GLAMORGAN Wanderers were 6-0 up in 15 minutes against Plymouth Albions at the Memorial Ground, Ely.

Former Welsh Youth International Andrew Phillips put Wanderers ahead after 12 minutes with a 35 yard penalty, and then fullback Phil Steele increased Wanders lead in the 15th minute with a magnificent straight penalty from the halfway line.

Albion who had lost only six of their 31 games this season, emphasised their current form when David Venables went over from a five yard scrum in the 20th minute for his 26th try of the season. Outside half Paul Carter converted easily.

Wanderers had an escape when Albion's centre, Brian Hain broke through to tackle on a 40-yard run. But flanker Sean Deasy failed to take Hain's difficult pass on Wanderers' line.

Phillips figured in two spirited Wanderers' counter-attacks but each was checked.

Underlining Albion's forward ability, they took four heels against the head, against Wanderers' one, in the first half.

STEELE POINTS SPREE

FULL back PHIL STEELE scored 12 points for Glamorgan Wanderers in their 16-13 win over Neath at the Memorial Ground in Ely today.

Steele, just back from South Glamorgan Institute's tour of the United States, struck twice in three minutes just before the interval.

He was up in support of scrum half Gerald Lewis to score an unconverted try and then landed a 45-yard penalty to give Wanderers a 7-0 half time lead.

Neath hit back with two tries by flanker David Morgan and wing Paul Morgan in the first four minutes of the second half. Neale Harris landed one conversion.

But the All Blacks' 10-7 lead was wiped out three minutes later after a brilliant break by Steele paved the way for hooker HUW DAVIES to score his first try for Wanderers. Steele converted.

Neath fell further behind when STEELE put over his second penalty goal.

But Neath outside half Ithel Davies, Steele's college clubmate, put Neath only three points behind with a penalty 20 minutes from the end.

Neath suffered a blow when their record scoring full back Neale Harris went off in the 61st minute with a leg injury.

On the up – some newspaper cuttings from my final year as a student, including mention of my goal kicking exploits. Ironically this was a skill that was to become a massive anxiety trigger later on.

College boys on parade – playing for Newport v Swansea in September 1983. Marc Batten taking on Shaun McWilliams with yours truly in pursuit – we had been the South Glamorgan Institute's back three the previous season.

TODAY'S TEAMS

NEWPORT				SWANSEA
Colours: Black & Amber				Colours: All White
Phil STEELE	15	Full Back	15	M. WYATT
Marc BATTEN	14	Right Wing	14	A. SWIFT
Phil BLIGHT	13	Right Centre	13	D. RICHARDS (Captain)
Justin ROBINSON	12	Left Centre	12	G. JENKINS
Tim HARRISON	11	Left Wing	11	S. McWILLIAM
Andy PHILLIPS	10	Outside Half	10	M. DACEY
Alun BILLINGHURST	9	Inside Half	9	H. DAVIES
John RAWLINGS	1	Forwards	1	K. COLCLOUGH
Michael J. WATKINS(Capt)	2		2	J. HERDMAN
Rhys MORGAN	3		3	G. JOHN
John WIDDECOMBE	4		4	B. CLEGG
David WATERS	5		5	M. GRIFFITHS
David FRYER	6		6	M. DAVIES
Wayne RENDALL	8		8	T. CHEESEMAN
Roger POWELL	7		7	M. RUDDOCK

Substitutes:

Phil PARKER
Andy POCOCK

REFEREE: G. SIMMONDS (Taffs Well)

The match programme from that game. It was one of my best performances in a Newport shirt – if only I could have bottled the confidence and self-belief I had at that time!

As the late, great Ray Gravell used to say, "Phil Steele, not a bad full-back ..." Showing England centre Richard Cardus a clean pair of heels against the Barbarians.

"... But not a f****g good one either!" In pacifist non-tackling mode against Mark Ring for Newport v Cardiff. Amazingly he actually did go down with this ankle tap.

The Newport squad that won the 1985 Snelling 7s. Mike 'Spikey' Watkins (with the trophy) was the best captain I ever played with. He also had an uncanny understanding of my psyche.

Another 7s tournament win – this time with Glamorgan County at the Cardiff High School Old Boys event.

WELSH RUGBY UNION

Headquarters: CARDIFF ARMS PARK

P.O. Box 22
Cardiff CF1 1JL
Telephone: (0222) 390111
Telegrams: Welrun, Cardiff
Telex: 498966

Secretary: Ray Williams

Our Ref:

Your Ref:

SJD/CAW/29(a)

15th November, 1983

O 656

Dear Sir

Re: FRANCE 'B' v WALES 'B' - 3rd December, 1983
    Bourg-en-Bresse

I have been instructed by the Chairman of Selectors, Mr. W.R. Morgan,
M.B.E., to inform you that you have been selected as part of the
Squad to prepare for the above game.

The first training session will take place on Sunday,
20th November, 1983, at the National Ground, Cardiff. You must
report to the changing rooms no later than 10.00 a.m. and you
should be free to leave at approximately 5.00 p.m.

I would remind you that at the Squad session you must wear the
official W.R.U. tracksuit and footwear which has been supplied to
you. Those players new to the Squad will be supplied with their
kit on Sunday.

In the event of you being selected as a member or replacement for
the Wales 'B' team you will be required to wear the red players'
sweater (provided by the W.R.U.) and grey flannel trousers (NOT
provided by the W.R.U.). These are to be worn for all travelling
between Wales and France, the journey to and from the game and the
return journey to Wales.

Further details with respect to Squad training and travel
arrangements will be issued on Sunday, 20th November, 1983.

In the event of injury you must notify either the Chairman of
Selectors on Bridgend (0656) 55555 Ext. 337, or myself on Cardiff
(0222) 390111 as soon as possible because failure to participate
in a session can seriously damage its quality. Failure to report
an injury resulting in non-participation in a session must be
regarded as a serious matter. Listed below are the home telephone
numbers of the Selectors which must only be used in the event of
any player being unable to contact either Mr. Morgan or myself.

        Mr. W.R. Morgan (Chairman) Bridgend 3665
        Mr. John Bevan   Port Talbot 883839
        Mr. T. Cobner   Talywain 773264
        Mr. C. Rowlands   Upper Cwmtwrch 830673
        Mr. R.H. Williams   Cardiff 68733

In the event of a breakdown or some such occurrence on the Sunday
morning you can contact Mr. W. Hardiman on Cardiff 390118 between
8.30a.m. and 10.00a.m. It is anticipated that any   injury
sustained on the Saturday will have been reported before this time.

All correspondence relating to the Welsh Rugby Union should be addressed to the Secretary

The rather quaint way players were informed of a squad call up – a formal
letter from the Welsh Rugby Union.

WELSH RUGBY UNION

Headquarters: CARDIFF ARMS PARK

P.O. Box 22
Cardiff CF1 1JL
Telephone: (0222) 390111
Telegrams: Welrun, Cardiff

Secretary: Ray Williams

Our Ref:

Your Ref:

XXXXXXXXXXXXXXXXXXX.
15 November 1983

P. Steele

Dear Sir,

I am sure you will be aware of the fact that the Welsh Rugby Union has
entered into a contract with Adidas to supply certain types of equipment
for Welsh National sides. The position is that any member of the Welsh
National Squad or member of any Welsh International,'B' International
or WRU representative team will be required to wear the kit provided
when participating in any official squad session or official match.

The Union has agreed that on the above occasions, all players shall be
required to wear Adidas Rugby boots or Adidas training shoes, Adidas
tracksuits and when a rainsuit is used, an Adidas rainsuit. It will
also be the responsibility of each player to ensure that this equipment
is in good condition, clean and bright.

In order that we may institute these arrangements with the minimum amount
of inconvenience and delay, it is essential that all potential National
Squad members should complete the attached form, giving the details which
are required.

If any player has any particular problem in relation to sizes or fit
etc., he should contact John Dawes, the Coaching Organiser, immediately.

I should be glad if you would complete the form, sign it and return it
to John Dawes, WRU Coaching Organiser at the above address, by return.
A stamped addressed envelope is enclosed.

Yours faithfully,

RAY WILLIAMS
SECRETARY

The 'Lord giveth and the Lord taketh away' letter from the WRU informing
players that they must wear the training kit supplied by Adidas. As soon as
they found out I was injured they refused to give it to me!

Steele shock for Newport

by Paul Abbandonato

NEWPORT full back Phil Steele has been ordered by doctors to miss the rest of the season — to save his career.

Steele, 22, was given the bad news by a specialist after an X-ray examination of the pelvic injury which has kept him out of action for the last two months.

The X-rays have revealed that there is still a lot of inflammation around the player's pelvis, and only complete rest until the summer will not clear up the problem.

If Steele were to start playing again before August, he would aggrate the injury still further, causing long term problems which would put his whole career in jeopardy.

It is a bitter pill for the Newport player to swallow, especially as he had just fought his way into the Wales B squad when the injury began playing up.

Steele said: "It is sickening. I thought things were going well but I'm back to square one now.

"I had already pencilled in two possible comeback dates but I've just got to forget about those now.

"I've got no option but to do what the specialist says. My career is on the line now and I can't take any risks. I've now just got to look towards August and aim to reestablish myself with Newport again.

"Luckily there are apparently sufficient signs

PHIL STEELE

on the X-rays to show that it will go providing I rest."

Steele, who was originally told that his injury would take only three weeks to heal, has not played since the game at Rosalyn Park on November 12.

By the time he does return to the game he will have missed five months of action. However, adding to the problem for the player is the fact that he is a PE teacher and obviously will find complete rest very difficult.

"Only people who have had this sort of injury really know how frustrating it is," Steele added gloomily. "You can't do anything really. It is not painful until I put any stress on it and then it begins to hurt."

The news about Steele is the latest hammer blow to a Newport side who have been riddled with injury problems all season.

A week does not seem to go by without somebody taking a bad knock, while the club have been without Colin Smart and Nigel Callard all season.

Adding further to the gloom was the news this week that leading points scorer Andy Phillips is out for six weeks with knee ligament trouble.

In Steele's absence Phil Parker, Alf Wainfur and now Nick Devonald have all been tried in the full back berth.

Newport were very unlucky to lose 34-29 at the Gnoll earlier in the season. Their pack dominated that day and it was only some extremely slack play by the Newport three-quarters which threw the game away.

Newport's back line consisted of Phil Steele, Marc Batten, Phil Blight, Mark Fenwick, Ian Howells, Keith James and Tony Coombs.

Although the latter two are still in with a chance of playing next week, only Batten of those seven can be certain of starting the game.

Batten scored three tries in the previous game, and it was probably that performance which did as much as anything to get him into the international reckoning.

Steele in injury setback

UNLUCKY NEWPORT full back Phil Steele, in the Wales B squad this time last year, will miss most and maybe all of the rest of the season with the knee ligament injury which has already laid him up for four weeks, *writes STEVE BALE.*

The 23-year-old schoolmaster had the knee taken out of plaster at Cardiff Royal Infirmary yesterday only to be told by a specialist that the injury had not healed at all. Now he has to wear a special knee brace for the next month, with an operation certain to be needed if he continues to make no progress.

"When I went to the hospital I expected to be cleared to start training inside the next couple of weeks, but I'll have to forget about playing rugby altogether for the time being," said Steele last night.

"If it's no better in a month I'll have to have an operation in the New Year. They could have operated immediately, but that would definitely have put me out for a season.

"Even if the brace works and my knee improves, the outlook doesn't seem too bright.

How the press told the story of my groin and knee injuries - what they didn't know was that the real damage had been done to my mind.

PEN PICTURES

Player: **PHIL STEELE**	Birthplace:	ELY, CARDIFF
Birthday: 3.6.61	Height: 6' 2"	Weight: 13st 4lbs

Education (Schools/College): MOSTYN R.C. H.S.; SOUTH GLAM. INST.

Previous Clubs (if any): GLAM. WANDERERS; SOUTH GLAM. INST.

Employment: SCHOOL MASTER

Hobbies: PLAYING GUITAR

Other Sports (if any): CRICKET, SOCCER

Favourite Sports Person: STEVE OVETT, BARRY JOHN

Favourite Entertainment: Listening to a good After-Dinner speaker

Favourite Meal: LAMB CHOPS & MINT SAUCE

Career to date: WELSH STUDENTS, GLAMORGAN COUNTY WALES 'B' SQUAD (1983)

Best Memory (Rugby-wise): BEING A MEMBER OF THE ONLY GLAM. WANDS' TEAM EVER TO BEAT CARDIFF (1982)

Worst Memory (Rugby-wise): NEWPORT v FIJI (1985) – A MATCH INFAMOUS FOR FOUL PLAY ON THE FIELD

Ambition: TO MEET GOD – BUT NOT JUST YET!

Pen picture in a Newport match programme. My 'Good Catholic Boy' upbringing shining through in my final answer!

Phil Steele BA (Hons) – July 1983.

With Liz, at our wedding - July 1985.

A lovely day with friends and family. My sister Ann who died tragically, aged only 37, is far right.

The bride and groom, with my great mates from college (left to right): Marc Batten, Darryl Richards, Gareth Francis, Ithel Davies (best man), John Morgan, Huw Gilson and Terry Jones.

Daddy and daughter. With four-month-old Bryony – it looks like we've both had to endure listening to some of my jokes!

Treasured photos and great memories.

Team Steele – with Liz, Bryony and mother-in-law Judith, who I still call 'Mum'.

Not a care in the world - with Liz on a Caribbean cruise in January 2009. Within six months Liz had died of a brain tumour.

Dad's proudest day – with Bryony at The Law Society in London after she'd just been inaugurated as a solicitor.

Mr. Steele the PE Teacher – with St. Mary's RC primary school's 7s team in 1990. Future Wales and Lions full-back Lee Byrne is back row, second from left.

To

mR Stelle.

It's very hard
    to say goodbye,
But here's hoping
    that you know
The warmest thoughts
    will be with you,
Wherever you may go !

Good Luck and
    Best Wishes

From
    Lu Byrne .

A collector's item! One of Lee Byrne's first ever autographs - this on my leaving card when I moved on from St. Mary's.

Sir seeks full-time career as a broadcaster

WHEN the school bell rings on a Friday afternoon, most children hope they have heard the last from their teachers until Monday.

However, for pupils from Lewis Girls' School there is no escaping their teacher, whose voice can still be heard over the airwaves on a Sunday morning.

Special needs teacher Phil Steele talks to thousands of keen listeners every week on his Radio Wales programme.

Phil Steele's big easy chat show has been aired over the last five weeks, and has attracted a wide range of guests.

"I am just like anyone else really. I just take in everything around me and write down one-liners, so I always have a lot to talk about," said Mr Steele.

Originally a PE teacher, Mr Steele, from Taffs Well, is a former first class rugby full-back for Newport.

"Teaching and broadcasting is much the same thing, they both involve communication with people.

"I do love teaching, but I would really like to get into broadcasting full-time if possible," said Mr Steele.

Mr Steele also keeps busy as an after-dinner speaker and match reporter for the BBC.

BY HELEN MORGAN

"I don't take life too seriously, and I get an awful lot of my material from the people around me.

"I always test everything out on my wife Liz and Bryony, my 13-year-old daughter. By the time I use it on the radio they have heard it 35 times," he said.

The radio show, *Phil Steele's Big Easy*, is aired on Radio Wales, at 10.45am every Sunday.

"The programme reveals what a diverse bunch of characters we've got in Wales. I love meeting and talking to people and finding out what they get up to.

"I have talked to comedian Rod Woodward, to a rugby widow in Nantymoel whose husband goes to the rugby club six nights a week, and Duke Leonard of the Man band, which is still going strong."

Mr Steele is hoping to attract former pupil Stuart Cable, drummer in the Stereophonics, to his show.

"I am still waiting for a note to explain why he didn't have his games kit in school!" joked Mr Steele.

RADIO STAR: Teacher Phil Steele ready to go on air.

A press article from 2001, when I decided to go part-time as a teacher.

One of these on the mantelpiece should keep the kids away from the fire! My first BBC publicity photo.

Steeley on stage (1) with Wales coach Warren Gatland.

Steeley on stage (2) giving a speech 'the big finish' with a song for the expats in Hong Kong.

Steeley on stage (3) holding court at a lunch at Penybont AFC.

20th
LUNCHEON
in honour of
St. David

HOUSE OF LORDS

Toast List

The Loyal Toast
Martyn Cozens Esq.
Sales Managing Director,
Coors Brewers Wales & West

'Messages'
Jamie Owen Esq.

'The Welsh at Westminster'
The Lord Chancellor, The Lord Falconer

'Wales'
His Excellency Mr. Masaki Orita
Ambassador for Japan

'St. David'
Phil Steele Esq.

'The Welsh and Their Friends'
The Lord Parry

Not bad for an Ely boy – the menu card and toast list from the St. David's Day Lunch at the House of Lords in 2004. There were so many famous people there that I was the only one I'd never heard of!

Ready for the off at a 'Worthington Wednesday' rugby forum with former Wales captains Kingsley Jones and Martyn Williams.

Sharing a stage with rugby legends is one of the joys of after-dinner speaking. This time it's the ex-Pontypool, Wales and Lions tighthead, Graham Price – the greatest Welsh forward I've ever seen – who made a record 12 consecutive Lions test appearances.

Sharing a cheeky glass of white wine with one of the most naturally funny men I've ever met in rugby, Derek Bevan. The first Welshman to referee a World Cup Final and a superb raconteur.

At Landsdowne RFC, Dublin with former Wales Grand Slam winning coach – and a man who shares my love of the guitar and Irish music – Mike Ruddock.

"Have you heard this one Jiff?" Talking tactics before hosting an event at The Corren Hotel, Laugharne with Jonathan Davies and hotel owner Peter Burnett.

Look at that shine – and the trophy looks good too! Ready to go for *Scrum V* pitch-side at Parc y Scarlets with the Pro12 league trophy.

One of the joys of broadcasting at Murrayfield is a visit to the Bill McLaren Suite – the media room dedicated to one of my great rugby heroes.

Always nice to meet a 'Grand Slammer'. With legendary Welsh actor and entertainer Dewi 'Pws' Morris (centre), star of the brilliant film *Grand Slam*, and *Scrum V* presenter Ross Harries (left).

I've always been a great lover of folk music, especially Irish folk, and for a while I headed up a group named Celtic Air.

'Imitation is the highest form of flattery.' With former Ireland and Lions hooker, and great character, Shane Byrne at the RDS in Dublin. I once asked Shane if he fancied coming out for a few beers post-match, to which he replied, "No Phil. I fancy coming out for a lot!"

Helping my old college mate, the former Glamorgan and England batsman Hugh Morris, with the painting at Vale Cricket Club, Bridgend as part of the NatWest CricketForce scheme.

Getting it straight from the horse's mouth. With the race horse named 'Scrum V' and his Welsh trainer, Tim Vaughan.

'There's Only Two Tom Shanklins!' Inspecting the synthetic pitch at Cardiff Arms Park with former Wales and Lions centre Tom Shanklin. I'm on the right – I think!

Finally getting to wear the sacred jersey in the Millennium Stadium's home changing room.

With my all time favourite full-back, Andy Irvine. This was a lot closer than most players ever got to him at Murrayfield during a brilliant career for Scotland and the Lions.

This guy wasn't a bad full-back either! With the Australian legend David Campese, while I was on tour as host of An Evening With Campo.

At an Usk RFC dinner with Kate and former Pontypool and Wales prop, Charlie Faulkner.

'Never come back in on the same day you go out' (1). Post-production meeting in Dublin with ex-Swansea and Wales no. 8 Stuart Davies and *Scrum V* commentator Gareth Charles. As well as being a great 'tourist', 'Charlo' is in my opinion the finest rugby commentator working today.

'Never come back in on the same day you go out' (2). With my good friend, the ex-Cardiff and Wales wing, Adrian Hadley and Gareth Charles on the 2013 Lions tour of Australia.

It's a tough job, but someone has to do it! A *Scrum V* half-time interview with Miss Carmarthenshire, in a hot tub at Parc y Scarlets.

It's amazing who you get to interview at pitch-side. This time it's Cardiff's Olympic gold medal winning cyclist, Geraint Thomas.

Punching above my weight (again)! Kate and I on our wedding day – April 2013.

With my great friend and best man – the ex-Swansea and Wales centre,
Kevin Hopkins.

My new family!

On honeymoon with Kate in Australia – at the Suncorp Stadium in Brisbane ...

... and the ANZ 'Stadium Australia' in Sydney.

I'm a proud ambassador for several charities. This time it's tea with members of the charity SHINE which supports people with Spina Bifida and Hydrocephalus.

With Kate's nephew Harry Thomas, who has Spina Bifida and plays wheelchair basketball for Wales U19s. Harry is a great inspiration and from whom I've learned so much about the challenges of living with a disability.

Mental Health Media
AWARDS 2009

Factual radio

Shortlisted

Clive Norling: Whistling in the Dark

BBC Radio Wales

Presenter: Phil Steele
Producer: Steve Groves
Contributor: Clive Norling

The award nomination certificate for my BBC Radio Wales programme about the former international referee, Dr. Clive Norling's battle with depression. We didn't win but thankfully, we didn't get too depressed about it!

Phil "I've had depression but I'm still smiling, and I'm still me" Steele, with Dr. Clive Norling.

room, for hours and hours, talking and chatting with each other. A day later, the doctor informed us that there was no hope and they would have to turn the machine off. I can't even describe how terrible that feeling was. Looking at him, lying on the bed, it appeared as if he was breathing and just sleeping soundly but in reality, the equipment had been keeping him alive. He had gone.

My sister had him baptised into the Catholic faith before the machine was turned off for good. I wasn't happy about that. I thought she had done it without his permission. If he'd wanted to be a Catholic, he would have made that decision himself.

My father officially died on Thursday 21 July 1988. At the inquest, there was no blame attributed to the driver of the car.

We buried Dad in the same grave as my mother. At least they were back together again. After the funeral, I thought about how this was now the end of an era. My mother and father had both gone and I would never see or speak to them again. Even though I was 27 and married with a child, a house and a career I had never felt as alone and vulnerable as I did, after the funeral wake, driving away from my parent's home in Ely.

6

Drinking at the Well and Speakeasy

' "Got an hour in you?" That's the question most asked by Steeley after a Scrum V broadcast as he looks for likely candidates to accompany him to the bar. He'll be the first there getting a round in, however large that round may be, and he'll be one of the last to leave having shared hours of storytelling, reminiscing and of course a joke for every occasion. Steeley genuinely loves people and rugby as is shown by the response he gets from players, coaches, supporters and committeemen alike. "Got an hour?" – I've always got time for Steeley and I don't know many who haven't.'

Gareth Charles
Broadcaster

About a year before the death of my father, I was paid a visit by two men from Newport RFC, the backs coach Roy Duggan and one of the senior players, a great character named Keith James.

They told me they wanted me to come back to play for Newport. Their full-back, Jonathan Callard, was by this time an established player – indeed one of the best full-backs around – but with nearly 50 games in a season, the club wanted a good full-back as backup. I didn't have to think too long and decided to make my way back to Rodney Parade.

I had a great welcome from the players and supporters, although by this time 'Spikey' Watkins had left following a disagreement with the club's hierarchy.

I played quite a few first-team games in my first season back and generally did pretty well. I was now 26 years of age and considered to be 'experienced'. Well, that was a misnomer to start with! So many times you hear commentators say, 'Oh, Dai Jones showing all his experience there." However, I found that experience didn't equate to confidence, it just meant being more aware of the pitfalls and things that could go wrong on the field. My first thoughts before a game were, 'What if I drop the first high ball?' or 'What if I miss the first tackle?' Invariably I didn't (well perhaps the tackle!!!) but it was only once I got on the field, and had caught that first ball, could I generate any sense of self-confidence. The chronic and crippling anxiety which had set in following the depression was by now in full flow.

For me, the changing room before a game was a place of anxiety where I'd be racked by self-doubt. 'Spikey' sensed that and knew how to build my confidence, but he had gone. I remember being at Eugene Cross Park, about to run out to play against Ebbw Vale in a big Gwent Derby. Glen George, a flanker who was now the captain following 'Spikey's departure, paced about giving it the old battle cry from Braveheart. I sat, petrified, in the corner, staring at the closed changing room door, having an attack of claustrophobia just five minutes before the start of a huge game, with thousands of spectators baying for blood outside. My mind started racing: 'What if the door won't open ... what if I get stuck in here.' I found it hard to breathe and felt trapped and sensed the walls closing in. Rather than psyching myself up into a frenzy with my teammates, I just wanted to get out of there and relieve the anxiety engulfing me. I had no idea why I'd starting thinking those thoughts. What was going on?

Goal kicking was another great source of anxiety and panic. If I was the goal kicker on the day, which I often was, particularly when playing for Newport Utd, the club's second XV. I dreaded it when the ball got down to the oppositions' 22-metre line. The panic would grip me. I kept repeating over and over to myself, "Please ref, don't blow for a penalty for us. Please don't blow for a penalty."

The shriek of his whistle felt akin to a judge donning the infamous black cap when pronouncing a death sentence. Inwardly I would mutter, "Oh God no ... a penalty."

As I walked up to take it, I could feel everyone watching me. In my mind, the people in the stands were all whispering about me, and their comments weren't positive. As I desperately tried to blank those thoughts out of my mind, I'd make a divot in the turf for the ball and look up. In front of me, the posts appeared to be moving closer together, the gap getting narrower and narrower. I had no option but to take the kick as quickly as possible in case the gap disappeared completely. I'd run up to kick and all I would be thinking was, 'Please let it go high and long,' so at least the crowd watching from the side would say that I missed but it wasn't a bad effort. Once these thoughts of doubt took over me, I was screwed. If a kick was successful I was hugely relieved but rather than me thinking, 'That's good, you've got your kicking boots on today Steeley,' the inner voice would be telling me, 'You were just lucky then. Just wait for the next one, you'll blow it – big time!'

What a difference a few years and a lack of confidence can have! At college, I would go looking to take the kicks. Missing them wouldn't cross my mind. I was young and full of confidence. I'd step up, and whack them over, and if I did miss, so what? I'd get the next one. But by now, my confidence was draining away and I was really suffering.

This now extended to getting anxious about travelling with the team to away games. I just couldn't bring myself to get on the team bus. I can only imagine the puzzled looks on the faces of my teammates and how they must have joked about it all.

It clearly wasn't healthy and I knew it. Instead of enjoying the *craic* with the boys, enjoying the feeling of the pre and post-match atmosphere, I climbed under my rock and refused to come out. I couldn't help it. In my mind, I wanted to ensure I could get back from wherever we were playing in my own time. I didn't want to be chained to the bus and governed by whatever time the players and committee decided to return home. If they wanted to stop off for a few beers, I didn't know if I could cope with it. I could feel the tension building up inside me just at the thought of us travelling away. I didn't want to feel anxious about it, so to remove the stress from that part of the equation I used to drive myself to the games. There were a few occasions where I got Liz to come with me in the car and I even dragged her up to London a few times. It wasn't right, I knew that.

Near the end of the 1988-89 season, Jonathan Callard left Newport to join Bath, a move which would eventually see him become the England full-back. This was great news for me, as being the 'next cab off the rank', I was in line to slot back into the first team as first choice full-back. Sure enough, I was soon selected to play against Pontypridd, scoring a try and racing 90 meters to make another, in a game in which the *Western Mail* described me as 'the veteran full-back'. I was only 27!

Despite my anxiety, I thought things were looking up, especially when it was announced that Newport would face Wayne 'Buck' Shelford's touring New Zealand All Black in a few months times, as part of their autumn tour. That was some carrot to dangle in front of a player in those days. To play for your club against a major touring side was the next best thing to winning a Welsh cap.

On the Tuesday following the Pontypridd game, I was at home when I received a phone call from a guy I knew from way back by the name of Windsor George. Windsor was now chairman of Llandaff RFC but had been the team manager for the combined Llandaff/Glamorgan Wanderers Youth tour to Canada, that I'd been on ten years earlier. He asked if I was available to be the guest speaker at Llandaff Rugby Club's end of season dinner. As the conversation progressed he told me he had seen me playing in the game against Pontypridd a few days earlier.

"Why didn't you come over and say hello?" I asked.

"I didn't want to disturb you," he replied and then told me how he'd brought a young lad with him, Matthew Silva from Landaff Youth, who'd just been capped by Wales Youth at full-back.

"Next time you come over," I politely suggested, "bring him along and introduce him to me. It would be nice to meet him. Maybe I could show him the ropes and put a good word in for him with the coaches," I added naïvely.

There was silence on the other end of the phone. Then he muttered, "Oh there's no need, he's playing for Newport against Bristol on Saturday."

"What?" I exclaimed in startled disbelief.

"He's been told by the Newport committee that he'll be playing Saturday, and that you're playing against Aberavon in the Monday evening game."

The phone went silent again. This time I was the one who didn't know what to say. I couldn't believe what I'd just heard. Here I was, being told by someone from outside the club, that I was being replaced by an up-and-coming youngster. Don't get me wrong, Matthew was a very fine full-back but that wasn't the point. There are ways and means of doing certain things, and this wasn't the correct way. For goodness sake, this was the great Newport RFC – one of the top clubs in the world.

I immediately went to see the committee and the coaches. Inwardly I was tamping but I decided to try and remain calm and collected. I adopted the demeanour of the classic bollocking I'd often given to kids in school. 'I'm not angry with you Jonny, I'm not even annoyed, but I am very disappointed in you!'

In front of the assembled hierarchy, I began, "You may think I'm not good enough or past it – that is your prerogative as a selection committee – but it would be preferable if I heard it first-hand from you that I'm dropped from the team rather than from the chairman of another club!"

The combined look of embarrassment on their faces was, well, embarrassing.

That autumn, as the new season got underway, despite training hard – as I always did – I was only given one first team game to press for a place in the side to face the All Blacks. When I failed to even make the bench for the big game I, as they used to say in the *News of the World*, made my excuses and left.

With hindsight it might have been better for me to have quit rugby after suffering the very first bout of depression in my early twenties. After all, it would have saved a lot of heartache and the frustration of knowing that despite giving something your best shot, mentally you're never firing on all cylinders and you'll always be swimming against the tide as a result. Perhaps I should have concentrated on my ever-growing after dinner speaking career or tried to get into broadcasting at that much younger age.

But rugby was in my blood. I had lived and breathed the game as fan, ballboy, player, teacher, coach and general anorak since the age of eight. Rugby was part of my soul and I wasn't ready to give up playing quite yet. As the great Scottish novelist, Robert Louis Stevenson put it, 'To travel hopefully is a better thing than to arrive.'

So, I continued my rugby journey by joining my local club, Taff's Well. It was the first time in my life I'd played for a village side, a real community-based team. Glamorgan Wanderers was a great club with fantastic fans but there wasn't a town or village called Glamorgan Wanderers and as a result it didn't really have a community spirit. South Glamorgan Institute was a college team – it couldn't be anything else – with players leaving at the end of their studies and never returning, whilst Newport was a big city team – a professional outfit in an amateur sport – where excellent players came from across Wales and beyond. Taff's Well was different. All the players more or less came from the village. I had never experienced that before. It was great to see the entire village turning out for cup matches, with the wives and girlfriends camped out in the club house after the match and usually staying there until the bar shut.

The camaraderie was amazing, with lots and lots of sing-songs after each game and I don't think I stopped laughing all the time I was there. I loved it. Even some of the mad things we had to do like 'flower eating' which was a new one on me. It was a 'boat race' with an extravagant twist. Racing against another team, we had to drink a pint as fast as we could, then bite the head off a flower and eat it: all done in the name of the *craic* mind you. I often saw players spewing beer all over the floor, spotted with bits of chewed flowers!

The sing-songs were renowned, usually lead by two great characters, Gary 'George' Davies and Elon Gough, who also played the keyboard long into the night. There was also legendary club hooker Mike 'Jed' Bonnetto whose party piece was singing *Lady in Red*, in the style of the 'pub singer', into an empty bottle of Budweiser. It was hilarious. I hadn't experienced a social side to my rugby like this since my college days at Cyncoed.

I'd lived in the village for four years before I played for Taff's Well. People knew me and I knew them but it wasn't until I wore the jersey and ran out to the field that I really felt part of it all. I probably got to know three times more people in Taff's Well within the first two weeks of playing for the village than I had in the previous four years of living there.

It wasn't all beer and flowers and sing-songs however. Although they partied hard, they played hard as well and the club had a fair bit of history to shout about. It was the club that had proudly started the careers of some Welsh rugby greats like Bleddyn Williams and Steve Fenwick. It was known as a club where up-and-coming players could progress to greater things if they were good enough and had the right attitude.

After a short while, I became a player coach, firstly alongside ex-Wales and Lions prop Ian 'Ikey' Stephens – himself an ex-Taff's Well player – and then former Bridgend and Wales B hooker Geoff Davies, who was to become a good friend. I was thrilled but I soon realised I wasn't a good coach. It wasn't part of my make-up. It was strange because I've always been a bit of an anorak when it comes to the game. I knew all the statistics – all the facts and figures, who played for whom and when etc. – but that didn't do me any good. To be honest, I was hopeless at coaching a senior team. I'd be the first to admit it. At times, I'd have to glance at the scoreboard to know what was happening.

My main problem was I struggled to read the game. I couldn't think those few steps ahead which was vital for a coach. My tactical awareness was non-existent, as I just couldn't see the 'big picture' of the match being played in front of me. I just didn't have it. What made matters worse was that despite coaching children in my job as a primary school PE teacher, I found it difficult to coach and develop adult players with totally different personalities and abilities.

On the field of play on a Saturday, I wasn't the captain but often the players would look to me for direction since I was a coach. The 'Un-Special One' would have been a good name to suit my persona.

"What shall we do Phil?" someone asked me during one game when we were losing.

I could feel myself panicking. "Oh I don't know...just chuck it out," I replied. I couldn't think of anything else to say or do.

It was all quite odd really, considering that when I devised the two-hour training sessions on wet Tuesday and Thursday nights, the players seemed to like them – although they did sometimes refer to me as 'Cone Man' because I always had a set of old traffic cones with me for the different drills. I found it quite easy to organise and run a good session of ball skill work and fitness for the boys – irrespective of how many players were there – but during the match itself, I couldn't think on my feet. I was never a thinker on the game, which is quite ironic since I actually work in that field now. Today, in my role working for the BBC, I normally have the best view in the house, but I still can't see the wood for the trees, as the saying goes. My job is to describe what is happening during a game, not to devise winning strategies.

During a match, I hear people like Jonathan Davies making a great point about some move or other and I think, 'Now why didn't I see that?' It's like I'm concentrating on one small aspect of the match, while someone like Jonathan can somehow see the bigger picture. I find it bizarre, that as a trained PE teacher, ex-player and student of the game, I lack that analytical mindset when it comes to coaching.

Steve's Fenwick's younger brother Mark, who was club captain, had a fantastic dry wit, and was a sharp cookie. He picked up on my lack of confidence on the pitch from an early stage and conjured up another nickname for me: 'Insecuricor'.

Good coach or not, I just loved the humour which bubbled up in the club. One of the funniest things I've ever heard on the field was when our prop – the 'hard as nails' Alan 'Bonehead' Jones – lost it completely, halfway through a tough match when our backs, me included, were trying to play a running expansive game. However, on this one day it wasn't going well, to say the least. The backs kept dropping the ball or knocking-on. I must admit I was one of the worst offenders.

Each time our forwards got up from a scrum they'd be shaking their heads because something had gone wrong yet again. Eventually, after another handing error, Alan got up from the bottom of a ruck, knackered and cheesed-off and called us all in for a team talk. We slowly walked towards him. "Come on boys for God's sake, what's going on?" he growled at us, before adding, "Boys, if I'm fighting four of them on the floor there must be a f*****g overlap somewhere!" He shook his head again and bounded off.

We had been royally told off. We decided to kick everything for the rest of the game instead of having 'Bonehead' on our case.

When I'd played in the first class game, I'm not sure if things like that went on; a mean, angry prop calling all the backs in to give them a bollocking. Perhaps it did and I wasn't tuned into it but I really found the humour in the lower divisions tickled my funny bone more than anything else. Those characters and situations will stay in my memories forever.

Another larger-than-life character at Taff's Well RFC was our very own club doctor, a lovely guy called Peter Grundy. He was also the GP for the village and was one of those doctors who always seemed to be moaning about how stressful his job was and how overworked he was. One Saturday, having sustained a dead leg after a tackle, I could hardly walk and needed some Ibuprofen anti-inflammatory tablets. In those days you couldn't just get them in the shops, you needed to see a doctor and get them on prescription. I asked him if he had his prescription pad with him.

He didn't, but told me he would leave a prescription behind the bar for me on the Monday night. Imagine that happening today! When I arrived at the club, still limping I must add, I called over the bar steward, Billy Simmons, and secretively whispered to him: "Billy, has Peter left a prescription for me?" I looked left and right in case someone overheard me.

Leisurely, Billy wandered behind the bar, picked up a pint glass and shouted, "Yeah here it is," holding up the glass which was rammed full of different prescriptions. There must have been enough prescriptions in there to satisfy all of the players, the committee and all of their wives. I soon found out it was easier to go to the rugby club to get treated than to go the surgery. It was one of those kinds of places!

I continued playing for Taff's Well for about two and a half years until, at the tender old age of 30, I decided to call it a day. I remember it was a lovely March afternoon; one of those bright, crisp days which was ideal for rugby. Normally I would have been looking forward to the game. Looking forward to packing my boots and shorts into my kit bag and heading off to the club house but, looking up the blue sky, for the first time ever I thought, 'Wouldn't it be lovely if I could take Liz and Bryony to the beach.'

Now every sportsman and sportswoman knows, once you are thinking more about taking the family to the beach on a Saturday afternoon instead of running about a field chasing a ball, your career is well and truly over. Good God, the next thing I knew, I would be merrily wandering around IKEA on a Saturday afternoon pushing a shopping trolley, and then what?

The warning signs were staring me in the face so I retired at end of that season. To be honest, I never missed the playing side from that day to this. As far as I was concerned, I had turned the page and was looking to move on to a new and hopefully more exciting chapter in my life. I just needed to find something else to do with my spare time.

What the whole Taff's Well experience taught me was what a real rugby club means to a village and how important a village team is to Wales. I'd loved the game since I was eight years of age but it took me over 20 years to find out what really holds together the fabric of Welsh rugby and, in a way, Welsh life. It was only then that I realised the scale of it, the huge numbers of people who did what they did for the love of the game; the players, the committee, the wives and the supporters. None of these individuals were getting paid and best of all, none of them ever expected to be paid in the first place. They did it week-in, week-out for the love of the game and the pride of the village. People like Dai Collins, the team secretary, who if you cut in half would have the club's colours of black and white running through him. There are characters like that in every rugby club in the world. Doing it for the thrill of seeing their beloved team run out of a Saturday and hopefully beating their local rivals before heading to the bar for a few drinks and a sing-song.

In my humble opinion, I think we are losing characters like that not just in Welsh rugby but in world rugby. Individuals who do things for the love of the game and nothing else. When the game turned professional that all changed. It had to happen of course. It had to go professional. It was ridiculous the way it was, especially compared to other sports like football and cricket. We were living in the dark ages. Kerry Packer was sitting on the side-lines ready to stir it all up by threatening to create a rugby circus. It was the kick up the backside the sport needed, but when professionalism did come it was ill-thought-out. It was often run by well-meaning but essentially amateur people who had no experience of professional sport. Rugby changed into a different sport altogether but was still run by the same people, who weren't prepared and were ill-equipped for what lay ahead.

In a way, the professional game totally took away what made rugby so special in Wales. The 'I want to play for my village' and 'I want my village to beat our rival village at all costs' mentality. The hardness and competitiveness in the game disappeared, as did the social side because many of the players were no longer representing their own clubs, villages or towns. It created a lot of mercenaries who were happy to travel anywhere – in their new sponsored cars – to play a game, collect their fee and head home. Very few players now played for the badge and the pride of their club.

Suddenly, every Tom, Dick and Dai expected to be paid. One week they were happy to play for the love of it. The next, they all thought they had turned into the All Blacks and demanded cash. To me it took away what made rugby special.

All the emphasis today is on the international game, and there are lots of people who think that's how it should be, but not me. It's about getting individuals – of every shape, size and background – out on that pitch and moulding them into a team. As the game develops, it seems now to all be about the professional game. The academy system is working, which is good for the professional game and good for the Welsh senior side, on the downside however, it sweeps up all the best players at 15 and 16 years of age and takes them away from their clubs and their mates. For example, if it had been me today growing up in Ely at 16, I would have probably gone into the Cardiff Blues Academy. I would have had a nice track suit, the kudos of being on the books of a professional team and filled with the (often false) hope that I would become a full-time professional. I wouldn't have been able to play regularly for Glamorgan Wanderers Youth and experienced the special bond that comes with growing up in a club culture. At the age of 18, they may have told me, like they do with most youngsters, that I wasn't going to make it, and I would have been cast aside. Like lots of teenagers today I would probably, at that stage, have just walked away from the game.

The maddening thing is, lots of these boys could have been good club players for lower teams and, who knows, they could have developed into much stronger players and bounced back and been top class. In my opinion we are losing so many potential players because of this system. Of course, a few make it to the very top – the Sam Warburtons of this world – but he is the exception not the rule.

It will be a massive problem in years to come. I can see, if this keeps on, in 10 or 15 years' time, hardly anybody will be playing rugby for fun. There will mainly just be schools – which are not playing anywhere near the number of games they did years ago – academies and the professional game. It will be similar to American football in the USA.

If you add into the mix the plethora of other sports and activities available to kids, plus parental pressure to give up the game at 16 due to it becoming too physical and, with student debt and harsh economic conditions forcing more young people to take Saturday and evening work, I sometimes fear for the future of the sport in Wales.

I'm not sure what we can do about it. We can't re-engineer society. Maybe it is just the way society is going. Maybe we just have to accept it.

However, I am encouraged by the fact that the WRU has appointed former Wales captain Ryan Jones to the board as Head of Participation. Hopefully that can help stem the haemorrhaging of players from the game and reverse the tide. He has a massive task on his hands and I wish him well. Anyway, time to get off my soapbox and get back to the plot.

Although my rugby career had come to an end I still continued to enjoy playing cricket in the summer. I scored my first hundred for Wenvoe CC, at the tender age of 28, against Southerndown; a team which included a young off-spinner called Rob Howley, who would later became a Wales and Lions scrum-half and international coach.

I had great fun playing for Wenvoe for 16 years. I've never met such an eclectic mix of characters of all shapes, sizes and abilities with each seemingly possessing his own unique idiosyncrasies. It truly was a team made up of the proverbial butcher, baker and candlestick maker. One character who stood out from the rest was a certain Mal Bowsher who became and remains a great friend.

Mal hailed from the valleys village of Abercynon and was a big bloke, both in body and personality. He loved to play hard on the field and enjoy life off it. Drinking in a round with him after a match was not for the faint hearted especially if it was his favourite tipple of 'Valleys Champagne' – also known as Strongbow cider! We used to refer to the experience as being in 'A Round With Malice', named after the TV programme hosted by the golf commentator, Peter Alliss called *A Round With Alliss*. Most people who went head-to-head with Mal usually found themselves, let's say, 'in the bunker' well before 10pm.

Mal's other amazing skill was his ability to use industrial language in industrial quantities, seemingly without causing offence. I remember one occasion when a few of us from Wenvoe C.C. went to Lords to watch a Sunday league match.

It was a quintessentially English scene; a beautiful afternoon with MCC members strolling around resplendent in their cream suits, Panama hats and distinct MCC ties. Mal and I decided to go for an ice cream at a van which was parked next to the famous Grace Gates – the main entry point to the hallowed Lords ground and one of the most iconic and sacred places in cricket. Suffice to say that Mal took a slight exception to the price being charged for the ice cream which he obviously felt was somewhat higher than Abercynon rates. At the top of his voice and in his finest Cynon Valley drawl he cried out in an anguished tone, "F*****g hell! How much? At least f*****g Dick Turpin wore a f*****g mask!"

For what seemed like an age the sound reverberated around the length and breadth of Lords. Cringing with embarrassment I wanted the ground to instantly open up and swallow us both. The various MCC members stopped dead in their tracks and swivelled around to stare at Mal, like a scene from a Wild West saloon bar when the pianist stops playing as the 'baddy' walks in. Mal didn't attempt to hide. On the contrary he stood there, large as life, as if daring anyone to admonish him. I had visions of being ejected from the ground at the very least and probably being arrested as well.

Then amazingly, everyone just carried on walking as if nothing had happened, as if to say 'Oh, it's ok it's only Mal from Abercynon, he's alright.' One or two of them even came over for a chat, as did the ice cream seller. That was Mal. I've never a known anyone in any walk of life with the ability to strike up a rapport and get on with people as has Mal.

Characters such as Mal and Ray Palfrey are so important in my opinion. They are the people who bring humour, warmth and colour to our lives and are vital in our families, workplaces and among groups of friends. I think they're known in management-speak as 'radiators', as they give out so much

119

positivity, as opposed to 'drains' who are the opposite. I would like to think that most of my family, friends and colleagues would have me down as a 'radiator' rather than a 'drain', which is strange given the fact that I've been dogged by so much negativity of thought for so much of my life.

I continued to play cricket competitively until my late thirties but having given up rugby at the age of 30 I needed to fill the void left by the game that had been a such massive part of my life.

Let me take you back in time to May 1984. During that month I was asked to attend an end of season dinner at my local club Caerau Ely RFC. They asked me if I would come along and give out a few awards. Feeling quite relaxed about the whole event, I even got up and told a few stories about my career and more significantly about the characters I'd met along the way: personalities like Charlie Faulkner, 'Spikey' and others. They loved it. It felt great to have such total command over an audience. They really enjoyed my speech and laughed in all the right places. It felt exciting, much better than scoring a try or hitting fifty runs at cricket.

After that I got invited to another club to give a speech, and then another. Pretty soon the word got around that this Phil Steele bloke wasn't a bad speaker at all. It suddenly opened up a brand new life for me. I didn't want payment; I was doing it just for the love of it. It didn't feel right to charge people for my services. It was all new to me. I would have spoken for a free meal and a couple of pints of shandy.

Then, in 1988 I got a call asking if I would speak at the dinner of South Wales Life and Pensions Insurance Association at the Angel Hotel in Cardiff. They gave me the grand sum of £75 for a 20 minute speech. I was over the moon. If truth be told I would have paid them to sit there and enjoy my speech – that's a feeling I still get now.

DRINKING AT THE WELL AND SPEAKEASY

The gig for the South Wales Life and Pensions Insurers went better than I could have planned and more importantly, it wasn't a rugby club crowd having their end of year presentation. This was a different ball game altogether, a completely different audience. It challenged me and made me think of different ways to approach my speech and to engage the audience.

Soon it became part of my income but like I mentioned earlier, I didn't do it for the money. Funnily enough, even all these years later as a seasoned and professional speaker, I'd still rather speak at a small rugby club for a few hundred quid and get a standing ovation because I'd gone down well, than get paid a four figure fee, but face a tough audience.

I became more and more confident the more diverse and varied the after-dinner speaking became. A lot of after-dinner speakers only flourish in their 'own' environments – a profession where they have previously worked – but I didn't seem to need that. It broadened my mind, increased my confidence and I soon widened my horizons by branching out into the golf and cricket circuits. My phone rung constantly with invitations.

The strange thing is, however, people ask me all the time, how can someone, who'd suffered from depression and anxiety for so long, stand up and speak so well in public? I'm not sure. I read a book once which listed the things people feared the most in life. Number three was financial ruin, second was dying and the one way out in front, the top of the pile at number one was speaking in public. The great comedian Bob Monkhouse once famously said that he'd spoken in public and died at the same time and that was even worse. I certainly know that feeling!

It didn't make much sense, did it? Here I was, a man who struggled with depression and anxiety, more than happy to stand up in front of anyone and do my thing. Of course I got nervous and still do. That's a primeval fear. We are basically social animals and as soon as we put ourselves outside of the group, in front of an audience or outside of our comfort zones, it can spell danger. Yet, when I get up to speak at a dinner it feels like the most natural thing in the world. At times it has been quite the opposite of what was going on in my everyday life.

In comparison, take someone like Neil Jenkins who, in his playing days, could switch off from everything and everyone in the ground and kick a conversion in the most hostile of circumstances. It came naturally to him, supported by years of practice and a fine-tuned mental strength, but put him on a stage in front of people to speak about how he did it and he would probably struggle. It was the opposite for me. When I was on the field and kicking, I felt anxious; I had demons casting doubts inside me. Yet standing on stage, in front of an audience, those demons were nowhere to be seen. I was the head of the orchestra. Nothing fazed me. Suddenly, doing something that people didn't expect me to do, held no fear for me at all: for once a case of 'Nerves of Steel' rather than *Nerves of Steele*.

I went to speak at functions hosted by the Round Table and Chartered Institutes of this and that, travelling all around the UK, and by the mid-1990s I was getting paid £200 to £300 per gig, which was good money on top of my teacher's wages. In 2004, I spoke at the House of Lords' St. David's Day lunch. Imagine that? How could I eat anything when I knew I was about to stand up in front of the great and the good of Welsh society. The Lord Chancellor at the time, Lord Falconer, was my warm-up act but the whole experience felt like the most natural thing in the world.

My bookings diary began to fill, soon I was doing 50 speaking engagements a year and it probably could have been more if I didn't have my teaching commitments. It was only my 'out of school' availability that held me back. I took the whole after-dinner speaking very seriously. I was focused and I practised. Beforehand I researched the profile of my audience, the age, the gender, the geographical area and any pressing topics. The last thing a speaker wants to do is to say the wrong thing at the wrong time. I've seen so many speakers who haven't bothered to do even a little research and have fallen flat on their faces. It's not a nice place to be, standing up and dying on your arse, let me tell you. Once is bad enough. I still have the scars.

I did have some sticky moments over the years. Once, at the Grosvenor Hotel on London, before speaking to the Chartered Institute of Purchasing and Supply – South East Branch – the compère introduced me by saying: "Ladies and Gentlemen. Here is one of Wales' finest after-dinner speakers ... Mr. Phil Steele."

Well. What a reception I got. Four hundred people, packed into the room, all making sheep noises at the top of their voices. I stood there for over 30 minutes doing my best. It was one hell of a tough gig and possibly one of the worst I've ever had. At times during my speech I wondered if I was facing the right way or if my microphone had been accidently switched off but, I was professional and I didn't let it upset me. Unlike times during my rugby career when, if I'd miss a kick it would shatter me for days, now I'd just get back up on my feet, like a good boxer, and carry on.

Another event at Loughborough Rugby Club sticks in my memory. I didn't go on until about quarter to midnight and you can imagine what condition some of the crowd were in. The usual sheep noises rained down from the rafters as soon as I came to the microphone. Luckily or unluckily for me, I was stepping in for Brynmor Williams who'd pulled out at the last minute. The compère introducing me didn't have a clue what was happening and introduced me with Brynmor's CV, informing the drunken audience that I was Phil Steele who had earned three Welsh caps and played three tests for the Lions. For one night only I didn't care about the sheep noises. I was a British Lion!

With some of the audiences I soon learned it was alright not to get the big belly laugh reaction to my jokes. Different crowds reacted differently. The most important thing was hopefully they still enjoyed it even though they weren't rolling in the aisles with laughter. Many ex-players, when they retire, try their hand at public speaking. They usually find it's not as easy as they think. Many ex-players are content to conduct 'Question and Answer' sessions at dinners, and while that has its place, it is not really after-dinner speaking, which I now consider to be a performing art.

Being a guest speaker to me is like getting invited to someone's house. There's an art to it, a skill. It takes lots of work. You need to be there on time, be suitably dressed, hopefully not drunk and know your audience.

It seemed to just come naturally to me, like my early days in school, when I loved to get on the stage and entertain. It wasn't all plain sailing mind you. It could be quite painful at times. Many a night, for example, I've sat next to the most boring chairman that God's ever put breath into. At times like that I've just had to grin and bear it – it's all part of the job – sitting there, smiling and pretending to be interested in how his brilliant first team have beaten Abercwmtomtit by a drop-goal in the last minute and how the women in the kitchen make the best sausage and chips this side of the Severn Bridge. It is all part of the show. You have to treat every function as it's the most important you've ever been to, which of course, for that particular club or organisation, it is.

Overall my philosophy on after-dinner speaking came down to one thing. I tried to make sure that whatever happened during the night, even if they didn't quite get my sense of humour, they would still say that at least I was a nice guy, a decent bloke and they'd enjoyed my company. If they actually liked my talk as well, that was a bonus.

Strangely enough it was a conversation at a speaking engagement that was to result in a massive change for the better in my life.

In the summer of 1996, I went down with a nasty virus which made me feel quite rough and lethargic. It lasted for a few months into the autumn then left me with a severe bout of post-viral depression. It was a really bad episode – only slightly less severe than the very first one I'd experienced when I'd hurt my leg, years earlier.

For a while previously I'd been taking an anti-depressant drug called Dosulepin and as the depression took hold I upped the dose until I was taking the maximum allowed.

Worryingly, the drug seemed to have little effect and I struggled through the spring of 1997 just trying to get by on a daily basis. I would be in tears before leaving for school in the morning then battle through the day as a teacher – frequently finding myself locking the classroom door for a quick cry in between lessons. It was horrendous. The only consolation was that the depressive feelings, thoughts and anxiety would tend to lift slightly during the day. I coped by trying my best to keep going, in the knowledge that by the afternoon I might feel slightly better, but I used to dread going to bed at night, knowing that I'd have to repeat the experience the next day.

In May 1997, I was booked to speak at the Newbridge Rugby Club's end of season presentation dinner.

I didn't feel very well as I got ready to go. I felt very anxious, as if I was waiting for something dreadful to happen; the awful feeling of impending doom that sufferers of depression will recognise so well. My mind had turned in on itself again.

After the gig, the aim was for me to travel down to Little Haven in Pembrokeshire to join Liz and Bryony at a holiday cottage we'd booked for the weekend. Ominously however, while driving up to Newbridge Rugby Club, I knew my mind was in a bad way. Not because I'd be going on stage – I was looking forward to that – but because the depression had taken over. Outside the rugby club, I sat in my car in a terrible state. I really thought that this was it, that I couldn't go in and perform. Using the club's payphone I called my brother John and asked him to come up and help me. I'm so grateful that he agreed and he was soon by my side. We talked for ages about all sorts of things, to calm me down and distract my mind. It worked. Well, it worked enough to get me into the club and to take my seat on the top table, with the committee and other guests. It was your classic rugby club dinner layout. A bit like a wedding, with a long top table at the front and a few tables adjacent to it packed with people.

The chronic anxiety however, was not giving up without a fight and quickly returned, gradually enveloping me in waves. Small ones at first but then the waves got bigger and bigger. I thought that, for the first time in my life, I was going to stand up in front of an audience and break down in tears. I sat there, watching the clock ticking steadily towards 'show time', and wanting the meal to last forever. Inside I was shaking but I tried to focus my mind. Perhaps other people would have made an excuse and left, but I had an inner strength and determination that made me stay. To divert my dark thoughts I started a conversation with the club secretary, a lovely man named Brian Wellington. Distraction is always the first form of defence during an anxiety attack.

"Who's where on the tables then Brian?" I asked, not really interested but trying desperately to ward off the demons.

"The first team are on that one," he pointed, "you probably

recognise them. The youth team are over there. Coaches, supporters there and near the back we have the medical staff."

My ears pricked up. "Is there a doctor here?" I asked. He nodded and pointed to one of the men. "I'll be back now," I said and headed for the table.

"Can I have a quick word?" I asked the doctor.

"Of course, what's wrong?"

"I'm not sure how to put this but I suffer from depression and I'm in the middle of a bad episode of it now."

And I was. I was teetering on the edge.

He didn't say, 'Don't be stupid,' or 'Pull yourself together.' Instead, as calm as a cathedral, he took me next door to a quiet room for a chat.

"What medicine are you taking?" he asked.

"Dosulepin – 60mg."

I'll never forget his reply. "That's the trouble with a fund-holding GP practice."

"What do you mean?"

"That's quite a cheap drug that can plateau out over time and stop having any effect."

He was right I'd seemed to be taking more and more all the time to seemingly little or no effect.

"Have you tried Paroxetine?" he asked.

I shook my head. "Right, as soon as possible go back to your doctor and ask him to put you on Paroxetine."

I thanked him and we walked back into the hall. The dark cloud had lifted from over me, the demons inside my mind hid away for another occasion and five minutes later I was up on my feet, doing what I did best, telling stories and making people laugh. It went down a storm.

Later that night, with a smile on my face, I said my goodbyes and drove to Pembrokeshire in a much improved state of mind.

A few days later, I went to see my doctor and he gave me a prescription for the tablets.

I realise that medication is not a panacea for depression and that for some sufferers it may make little or no difference. I also know that there are other forms of treatment such as counselling and Cognitive Behaviour Therapy – which can be highly effective in the treatment of depression – but from personal experience I have to say that the drug Paroxetine had an incredible effect on me. It wasn't an overnight miracle cure but within a week or two I gradually noticed that I became less anxious. It was a strange feeling at first because as I'd suffered for so long, a state of anxiety had become almost normality for me. At first it seemed too good to be true and I half expected to wake up one morning with the anxiety having returned with a vengeance.

Eventually I grew more assured and confident that the condition was now under control. It was an exhilarating feeling and I now seemed to be a completely different person. It was as if I'd thrown off a heavy restrictive overcoat, which had now been replaced by a T-shirt and shorts in which I could move freely for the first time in years.

One of the unwanted side effects of the tablets was that I quickly gained weight, which wasn't ideal as I'd always prided myself on my fitness, but that was a small price to pay for the priceless state of a peaceful and satisfied mind. For the first time in years I wasn't having to deal with constant anxiety.

That night in Newbridge proved to be the turning point that changed my entire life.

7

Special Kids, Special Times

'There are four things you can be sure of when you are Phil Steele's friend. The first is that he'll make you laugh, even when there must have been times when humour was hard for him to find. The second thing is that he loves it when you make him laugh – this is no one-way comedy show. The third thing is that every time you see him, the warmth of his welcome makes you feel like a King. Hundreds of people in rugby clubs all over the globe will have felt it too. The fourth thing is that it's all genuine. The Phil Steele you have a curry with is the same one you see on the television. He's a real man with real values like loyalty, playing fair and good manners – those are things you can't fake and it's why so many people are proud to call him their 'friend'.'

Richard Thomas
Wenvoe Cricket Club

After about eight years teaching PE, I must admit I got bored. Not with the concept of teaching entirely, but just doing Physical Education for six hours a day.

What changed my mind?

I think I just got fed up with living my life, day-in day-out, in a tracksuit while watching kids chasing a ball around a field in all kinds of weather. I seemed to be on a constant treadmill. A routine which consisted of taking training, organising games, taking phone calls about players, worrying if the pitch and the bus would be ready on time and all those kind of basic things.

Whilst I admire all those PE teachers who've dutifully served their schools and their pupils – where would be without them? – it took its toll on me. I seemed to be getting old before my time.

On the other hand, I knew I had more to give to the teaching profession. There was a lot more I could offer – I just needed a new challenge. All through my career I'd always got on with those children labelled, incorrectly in my opinion, as the 'not so bright' or 'slow learning'. I've always believed that the educational system was at fault and had let those children down: they just needed to be shown respect and to have been taught in a different way.

Helping these sort of kids became my new challenge so I took a two-year diploma in special needs teaching at Newport University. To be honest, it nearly killed me doing my full-time teaching job and then going off to lectures for two to three hours most nights. It was tough going, but worth all the pain. I was determined to make a go of it. I even completed my assignments on time and by myself. I knew I'd matured and become more professional because when I was a young student at college, I'd always leave coursework or revision until the last minute. Typically, the night before a deadline, a gang of us would head down to the Claude pub in Roath for a few 'liveners', to get the academic juices flowing, and then we'd head off to one of the boy's flats and take it in turns to write bits of our assignment. We would all 'mix and match' our work, hoping the lecturer wouldn't notice, but now as a mature student and funded by the local authority, I took my work much more seriously and was far more focussed. I knew exactly what I wanted to do and more importantly, why.

SPECIAL KIDS, SPECIAL TIMES

It all paid off because I quickly found a job teaching special needs children at Lewis Girls' Comprehensive School in Ystrad Mynach. I taught the 11 to 16-year-olds in five separate classes, with about 10 kids in each class. It was exciting and new but scary at the same time. They were a real mixed bag of children with varying needs – some with learning difficulties or severe learning difficulties, and others with emotional and behavioural difficulties (EBD) – and I didn't know what would happen from one day to the next. I ended up teaching a variety of subjects including: Maths, RE, English, Geography, Personal and Social Education and a bit of Music here and there.

In a blink of a board-rubber, I went from being a specialist sports teacher, walking around in a tracksuit all day, to becoming a 'jack of all trades', but I loved every minute of it.

Each lesson was wonderfully unpredictable and seemed to take me and the pupils on a winding path of its own. I'd prepare a geography lesson and end up doing something completely different on the day or just sitting there with the kids and talking about life. It was that kind of environment. It wasn't a classroom for reading out quotes from text books but it proved to be so rewarding. Just seeing one of the quiet ones who, in year seven, wouldn't talk to anyone, but by year nine, had really come out of their shell, and start to feel good about themselves – that was a great feeling and it provided all the reward and incentive I needed.

My aim was to try to be a stable role model in their lives, for an hour a day. A number of them came from very tough backgrounds, who'd had difficult upbringings for a whole host of reasons. Most of the time I saw myself as more of an actor than a teacher. Today I'm a fully paid-up member of Equity, the arts and entertainment union, because of my public speaking work, but I could have earned my Equity membership for my

131

work teaching those kids. I had to act every emotion under the sun, from surprise to anger and from sorrow to joy. You name it, I acted it every day. It was like being on the stage.

It was immensely satisfying and I just adored those kids. The fact that most of them came running to my class told me that I was getting through to them and they enjoyed what I did. I wouldn't have swapped them for the school's other pupils for a moment. These were the kids who, I was told on many occasions, couldn't be taught because they didn't want to be taught, so it was very gratifying that they couldn't wait to get to my class for a few hours a week. It may be because I tried to show them respect and let them have a voice of their own.

Funnily enough, my guitar was my most important piece of equipment in the class. I used it for everything from musical numbers and word games, to just chilling-out and singing songs for them. I'd even make up verses for them and encourage the kids to sing along.

"Please sing that song sir," one girl asked.

"Which one, Alison?"

"The love song about the spring, sir."

I would smile, then pull a pretend sad face before singing,

"If the mattress should collapse my love, I'll see you in the spring."

The kids used to love it.

I was amazed but also sad to see how some of the other teachers just didn't have the same rapport with them. They simply didn't have the patience, yet patience was everything. The whole idea was to make them feel relaxed, so I adjusted my level to match theirs and became one of them. I found it quite disturbing how some teachers, for all their academic ability and training, just couldn't do that.

I could. It's a gift I've been told. Lots of individuals in life have that gift. Some can get soldiers to go into battle whilst others, like 'Spikey', could get players to run through brick walls for the cause. They possess that special ability to make people feel at ease and get the best out of them. As far as I was concerned, it wasn't about the kids being good at the subjects, it was about them feeling good about themselves and feeling excited about the world. It used to cost me a fortune in boxes of the mini-chocolate bars, I bought as prizes for the many games I invented, such as 'Maths Bingo' and 'Times Tables Buzz'.

The trick was to be creative. To think of new ways to get them involved and for them to not realise they were being educated whilst they enjoyed themselves. I used to get people up from the BBC to visit and talk to the kids about all kinds of things. We used to take the year eight 'Special Class' camping to Three Cliffs Bay on the Gower coast near Swansea. I recall one kid splashing about in the water and telling me she couldn't get over how cold it was and that it tasted salty. It then struck me that she had never been to the seaside before.

Every summer I'd take the year seven class to Cardiff for the day. My pal Mike Gibbons, another Taff's Well man, was Director of Tours at the Millennium Stadium. He would allow me to park the school minibus in the bowels of the stadium, at the exact spot where the Wales team bus parks, and then take us into the changing rooms and around the stadium on our own special tour. Mike probably thought little of it but his small act of kindness helped my pupils to feel important for once. You couldn't put a price on that. Then we would pop down to Cardiff Bay for a boat trip. It was brilliant seeing these kids soaking up their new surroundings like sponges. They came alive and asked questions about everything they saw.

Back at school they talked about it for weeks. "Sir, remember when you took us to Cardiff and we went on that ship sir....it was great wasn't it, sir!"

It was during my time as a special educational needs teacher that I had the most rewarding day in my educational career. The funny thing was, it was nothing to do with pupil achievement, exam results, or school inspection reports.

One Friday I was at the Cardiff International Arena, hosting the Honda Hall of Fame Rugby Dinner. It was a packed house with over 600 people there. While Peter Karrie was singing on stage, I tried my best to wolf down my dinner before getting back up on stage to continue compèring.

Suddenly, behind me I heard a booming voice, "Phil...Phil... Mister Steele...do you remember me?"

I looked up and came face to face with Welsh rock star, the late and great, Stuart Cable. I had taught him many years before in the comprehensive school in Aberdare but by now he had become famous as the drummer with one of the world's top rock bands, The Stereophonics.

Even though I had to tell him to stop calling me Mr. Steele, we talked like we had been the best of mates forever. To cut a long story short, I asked if he did anything with schools. Without a second's hesitation he said, "What do you want Phil? I'll do anything for you." This was a guy who'd played to massive audiences all over the world and had played drums on several number one selling albums.

I told him about the girls' school and my special needs kids, then asked him if he would come along and meet them. "Not the whole school," I added, I didn't want to frighten him off, "just a special thing for my special kids."

"I'd be delighted," he said, pulling out his electronic device to fix the date. "How's the 18th December looking sir...sorry Phil?"

"Great!" I said, "that's the last day of term before the Christmas break."

134

He gave me his mobile number and his email address. I will always remember it – thedukeofcwm.com! Who would have thought that he would one day become a 'Duke'!

The following Monday, I informed the headmistress, a delightful lady named Dr. Sue Noake, that he was coming. She was a massive music fan and loved The Who. To tell you the truth she was more excited than anyone that Stuart was coming. I told the head girl and the deputy head girl that I needed them to do a 'meet and greet' at 10am the next morning.

They rolled their eyes, probably assuming it was going to be a local dignitary, some boring old guy in a shirt and tie.

"Who is it, Sir?" they asked.

"If you must know, it's Stuart Cable from The Stereophonics."

That was it. They could hardly speak. "Can we bring some CDs and stuff for him to sign, sir...please...please?"

"Of course." I said and they raced off excitedly.

The next day, over the tannoy system, the head of department told all the pupils from the special needs classes to report to my room immediately after registration.

Classroom 72, my classroom, was a run-down, second-hand terrapin that leaked badly and you could almost put your foot through the floor. I sat all the kids down and told them to be quiet. I didn't smile. They thought someone had upset me and they were all in for a row.

"First of all, you're not in trouble, any of you." I assured them. "It's Christmas and no one gets in trouble at Christmas." In my mind I was now on stage, so my acting kicked-in. I was the opening act getting the crowd warmed-up. I launched into the big intro.

"You know what I say girls, about when you leave school and become whatever you become, and the best thing for any teacher is when they bump into you in the street, years later, and see how well you've done. Maybe you will be married and have a family, a good job and a nice house." They all nodded. "It would be great to see how you have got on in life. When I first became a teacher I taught PE in a school in Aberdare, and I used to teach this lad who played hooker in my rugby team. He was a lovely boy and always tried hard in PE and other lessons, but his hobby was playing the drums and I told him that if he worked hard and practiced his drumming he might, one day, play in a band. And do know what girls? He did work hard, became very good at playing the drums and joined a band you've all probably heard of."

The kids looked at me incredulously. You could almost hear them thinking, 'Mr. Steele has lost it, big time.'

"They're called The Stereophonics." There was an audible gasp from the kids. "And guess what? He's outside the door now. Come in to Room 72, Stuart Cable!!!!"

Right on cue, Stuart sauntered in. I will never forget it. A smile on his face like a half moon; his unruly hair all over the place and wearing the his rock star's garb of denim jacket, denim jeans and cowboy boots. "Hey...Mr. Steele, how are you?" he exclaimed, in his booming voice, before enveloping me in a bear hug. He turned to the gaping-mouthed children and said, "How's Mr. Steele treating you? He was a hard teacher in my day. He used to shout at me all the time!" before bursting out laughing.

The kids went crazy. I'd already got his photo from the internet and had loads of copies printed off for the girls. Fair play, he signed every single one of them. A few girls had some extra photos and kept coming up and saying, "Can you do another one for my Auntie Mary" or "my sister?"

When we'd all settled down I started a question and answer session with them and Stuart, and it was brilliant. If it had been a 'mainstream' class I'd have expected a host of good, but standard questions like, 'Why did you decide to be a drummer?'

or 'What are your musical influences?' but my kids were special, as the first question illustrated.

"Mr. Cable. Do you know Robbie Williams?" With a twinkle in his eyes, Stuart replied, "Of course, I know Robbie. I know him well. He came to my stag night in Aberdare. They wouldn't let him in the top club because he wasn't a member," he joked and then he told them the story of how Robbie had phoned Stuart's house when he was out and Stuart's wife, thinking it was someone from Aberdare messing about, hung up.

The life of a rock star hey!

An hour later and after what seemed like a million wacky questions, all answered beautifully by Stuart, I walked him up through the yard to the headmistress' office for a cup of tea. Once again, he sat there – patiently and attentively – signing stuff for her and the head girl and deputy head girl. Within 30 minutes, to paraphrase the title of The Stereophonics' first album, 'Word Got Around' that Stuart was in the school.

When it was time for him to leave, it was like Beatlemania at Heathrow airport. In front of my eyes, the so-called cool, older kids of the school, stood screaming and going absolutely hysterical.

One girl shouted out, "Oh my God! It's him." Then she reached forward to touch him as if he was Jesus, tears rolling down her face.

I finally got him to his car and, with a quick wave, off he went.

However, the main part of the story and why it was so important to me, is because it taught me a huge lesson. A degree in Physical Education, a Postgraduate Teaching Certificate, a Diploma in Special Needs Teaching, years spent at college, hours of lectures, essays, assignments, exams and tests could never prepare me for what I was able to do for my pupils that day.

Because of Stuart's kindness, my kids – the special needs kids, the snotty nosed kids, the ones who got bullied, the un-cool kids – were for once in in their lives walking around that school yard like they were the 'Queens of the Prom'. They strolled about with the signed photos of Stuart clenched in their hands; the photos which he'd signed 'to Julie', or 'to Helen' or whoever, 'Best Wishes and lots of love, Stuart Cable.'

For once, all the other pupils in the school were envious of my kids. For that hour, or morning or for the rest of the week, my special needs children were the important ones for once. I still get emotional just thinking about it.

That was more important to me than anything I've ever done in my whole time in education and it was nothing to do with education *per se*. It was just about being human and treating the kids the correct way. It was an honour to be able to provide them with such an experience. I bet they still haven't forgotten about that day – Stuart didn't and neither will I.

I'd been at Lewis Girls' School for about three years, and was beginning to accept the fact that I'd probably spend the rest of my working life as a full-time teacher in the classroom. I had no ambition to become a senior manager, an assistant head or deputy head. The after-dinner speaking was going well and I was reasonably content but I knew deep down that teaching, despite the feel good factor that it offered, was not totally fulfilling me. I knew somehow that there could be more to life. A chance conversation with Gareth Davies, the ex-Cardiff, Wales and British Lions outside half proved to be the catalyst.

Gareth was Head of the Sports Department at BBC Wales and told me that as BBC Radio Wales were now covering the eight Welsh Premier League games every Saturday, they were on the lookout for reporters. He asked me if I was interested. I said I was, and soon had an invitation to go for an audition.

A few weeks later I received a letter to say they liked what they heard and definitely wanted to use me in the future – step aside Bill McClaren, Phil Steele was in the house! I was excited. I even practised in my room, using an empty lager bottle as a microphone.

I didn't hear from them again for 18 months or so and thought my chance had come and gone when, out of the blue I got a call from a radio producer, Rob Thomas, in August of 1995. He'd seen my name on the list of possible reporters and wanted to use me. By that time I was also doing a bit of work for the Mid-Glamorgan Press Agency, writing reports on rugby matches, so had gained more experience and knowledge and was feeling really confident about my abilities as a reporter.

I jumped at the chance. My first game was Newbridge against my old club Newport, in September, and I loved it. I felt so comfortable and got a real buzz from the first minute to the last. I'd decided to put my own spin on my reports, as I didn't want to simply repeat all the old rugby clichés that were boring and overused. I didn't want to be just become another rugby reporter. It was important to put my own twist on it: to get the listeners to picture the game through the eyes of Phil Steele.

Unlike when I coached, or tried to coach – when I couldn't see the game playing out in front of me – I discovered that a reporter didn't need to. I quickly discovered that commentating just required me telling the listener what I could see and hear. I didn't need to second-guess what was coming next, that was left to other people. Not needing to read a game proved an advantage for a change and I didn't need to be technical, as I always had someone beside me in the commentary box to do that.

When there was a break in play I could turn to my colleague and simply ask, on behalf of the listener, "What happened there?" or, "Why did the scrum-half do that?" The other guy was the one who analysed the game. I was there to deal with the simple facts, not the theories. I liked that. I liked that a lot.

Watching a game as a reporter is completely different to watching it as a supporter or a coach. Even down to, as the game draws to a close, preparing your summing up – the story of the match – knowing you've only got a minute of air-time to tell the story of the game. As the seconds ticked away I'd be thinking: 'Don't go and score now and blow it. I've got my report. I've got my headline. I've got something really clever to say!

I also tried to bring my own sense of humour to the role. Nothing too fancy, just the same type of traditional Welsh humour and turn of phrase I'd heard in hundreds of Ralgex-infused dressing rooms for most of my life. I took my new reporting role very seriously and continuously worked at it. I even kept a notebook, into which I'd jot down ideas throughout the week leading up to the game I was covering.

Being the newcomer to the team I didn't get many of the big glamour ties featuring the teams at the top of the table and soon became a permanent fixture at the lower level games. I think I spent most of that season at Abertillery Park – Yes! Abertillery were in the Premier League then – dressed like an Eskimo, but they always gave me a warm welcome and something nice to eat. I quickly learned that it did not matter who the teams were, or what the quality of rugby was like, it was the experience I was gaining that was important.

During that same season I took a call from the BBC. "Phil, do you know anything about football?" To be honest, apart from watching Match of the Day on a Saturday night, my knowledge of football had got pretty rusty. I didn't want to say that I'd played for the cub scouts and a season or two with a Sunday team in Cardiff, or confess that the last game I'd been to see was Cardiff City against Luton Town at Ninian Park in 1971.

Being a good professional, I told him I loved it and that football was in my blood. He believed me and I was asked to cover the Swansea City v Rotherham Utd game at the Vetch Field the following Saturday. 'Good God!' I thought. 'What do I do now?'

It was an awful, damp, cold November afternoon with the wind blowing in from Swansea Bay. The steward showed me to the North Bank and pointed to a huge, old, rusty gantry.

"Up there," he said and walked away. I'm sure there was a little smirk on his face.

I looked up at this thing and thought it was a mistake, or they must be playing a joke on the new kid on the block. Alas no. I left my kit bag with all my essential equipment, like the microphone and my flask, at the bottom of the gantry and climbed up the metal ladder steps. It should have been condemned, never mind be home to a reporter on a cold winter's day. When I got to where I would be positioned, I had to lower a rope down and then climb back down the steps, tie my bag to the rope, climb back up and only then could I pull my gear up. I felt like I was on some kind of army manoeuvre.

To make matters worse, the game was absolutely terrible. I'd seen better matches on a Sunday morning in the park in Cardiff. As a matter of fact, we used to have better games than that on that little tump of grass when I was a kid living in Ely.

Chris Stuart, the presenter of the sports programme, cued me: "It's Swansea against Rotherham at The Vetch. Phil Steele is our man there. How's it going Phil?"

"Well Chris, its nil, nil. If fact it's very nil, nil. The only excitement has come from a shot on goal from 25-yards by

Swansea defender Keith Walker, which was about as accurate as a builder's estimate!"

It was the truth. There was nothing much else to say about it. I believed my report had summed up the match perfectly, had hopefully informed the listening public how dreadful the game was and how lucky they were to be somewhere else.

As the game went on, I couldn't help but see the funny side of it and I actually started to enjoy it. Even though I was stuck up on a 30-foot gantry with only the freezing weather for company, I began to warm to it.

Chris kept coming back to me from time to time, "How bad is it now Phil?"

"Chris, there are 22 tins of paint in the stand watching the players dry," I joked. Chris burst out laughing.

When it was over I packed up, lowered my stuff down the gantry and headed home. I knew I had done my best and now I'd go back to reporting on rugby, but for some strange reason the 'powers that be' at the BBC loved it. They liked the fact I told it like it was and with humour. The game had been awful and that's how I'd reported it, without trying to 'flower it up' as an exceptionally exciting match.

A short while later, I took a call from another radio producer who said he'd been given my name as one of BBC Wales' expert football reporters, and wanted to know if I could could cover the upcoming game between Exeter and Cardiff at Ninian Park, for BBC Radio Devon.

It felt quite odd, as an Ely boy, to report on the match from the viewpoint of the opposition but it was a great learning curve and I just hope that the Devonians understood my accent!

Pretty soon I began to receive requests, from other BBC stations around the UK, asking me to report on their local teams when they were playing in south Wales, against either Swansea or Cardiff. By that stage I didn't mind which station it was, as I was now getting regular air-time and improving as a reporter. The money wasn't great but that wasn't the point. I regarded it as an apprenticeship – a chance to hone my skills. It didn't matter where I was, it was still my voice coming out of the same box as proper stars like Terry Wogan! My parents would have been proud.

On the rugby front, in 1999 the BBC lost the contract for televising club rugby to ITV, so I spent most of the season reporting on football's League of Wales, covering matches between teams such as Port Talbot against Carmarthen. So whilst I'd previously moaned about the standard of football from the gantry at The Vetch, I was now reporting on games with only a man and three dogs for a crowd!

Again, staying positive, I used to read up on the town or the village, and try to pass on a bit of knowledge to the 'millions' listening. To be honest I tried to do anything to make the match appear more exciting,

"Welcome to Aberystwyth, the University town of the Prince of Wales, as the home side take on Caernarfon, the town where he was officially invested. Let's hope it's a game fit for a prince."

I like to think that I began to get a reputation as someone reliable and competent, two of the most important qualities in a freelancer. Also as someone who was a bit different, someone who was humorous and quirky.

Towards the end of the 1990s I had another big surprise when I was approached by a producer at the BBC, who'd heard about my after-dinner speaking and that I could play the guitar and sing. I was told that Radio Wales was about to launch a new Saturday morning sports programme called *The Back Page* and would I consider writing and performing a humorous topical song each week.

Of course, without thinking, I jumped at the chance even though I couldn't read or write music. *The Back Page* was scheduled to run for 30 weeks and I was still a full-time teacher. Preparing for that first show I had that familiar, 'Oh no. What the hell have I let myself in for' moment.

Like a true trooper, I soldiered on. The song for the first show was a little ditty about Glamorgan's cricket team, which was poised to win the County Championship for only the third time in their history. The song was entitled *Go Glamorgan*:

Go Glamorgan
You're Wales' sporting pride
Let them all in England know
You're the greatest cricket side
Here's to Watty, Cottey, Hughie, Matthew and the rest
Go for it boys and show the world Glamorgan are the best

It seems to go down well. I was up and running!

Not being able to read or write music I'd compose a melody in my head, try it out on the guitar, record it on an old cassette recorder and simply learnt it. Sometimes I'd lie awake in bed and, at 3am, eventually a melody would pop into my head. I'd get up immediately, record it and then go back to bed. I even bought a rhyming dictionary to help me compose the verses. My method wasn't quite in the Lennon and McCartney class of song-writing but it seemed to work for me.

The 30-week run nearly killed me. There are only so many chords and rhythms one can use but the feedback was good and it opened more doors for me. That autumn, when Wales hosted the Rugby World Cup, another producer wanted me to perform on a nightly programme, broadcasting live from the Slurping Toad pub in Cardiff. The show was to be called *The World Cup Experience* and he wanted me to do a similar thing as *The Back Page*, but this time he expected a new song every night for the duration of the tournament.

"Every night?" I spluttered, over a coffee.

He sensed my concern, "OK, how about a Monday and a Friday. You can sing two songs in each show. On the Monday you'll be looking back at the previous weekend and on the Friday you'll be looking forward to the coming weekend's matches. Just four songs a week."

Without considering the amount of time and effort it would take, I agreed – hey, that's show business – what else could I say.

Overnight, I transformed into the Welsh version of Val Doonican – woolly jumper and all – but that was stress, let me tell you. Nothing summed it up as much as the day when Wales played Samoa. Without that little thing called hindsight, I'd written one song about how Neil Jenkins was going to break the all-time international points scoring record during the match and another clever little ditty about Wales beating Samoa and coasting through to the quarter-finals. With everything in place, all I had to do was go and watch the game at the stadium, stroll over to the pub where my guitar would be waiting, sing the songs to a happy crowd and enjoy the rest of the night. What could possibly go wrong?

Well something went drastically wrong that not many people saw coming. The South Sea Islanders deservedly beat Wales. The whole ground and the nation stood in stunned silence but the result was secondary to me. While everyone was moaning about how we lost the match, I was thinking, 'Oh bloody hell. My clever little ditty doesn't work anymore, and I've only got 90 minutes to write a new one!'

In between walking from the ground to the pub, I was trying my best to compose a new tune, with lyrics, in my head. What didn't help was the amount of people stopping me to ask what I thought of the game, but I didn't care about the result by then. I had more important things to worry about. In time of panic,

145

the guitarist's best trick in his guitar case is to strum along to a bit of 12-bar blues, so that's what I did and, miraculously, a song and a tune popped into my head. I called it *The Interception Blues*, because Samoa had scored two interception tries in the game. I can still remember the chorus:

> *I've got The Interception Blues*
> *Don't you throw one or you'll lose*
> *Yes those men from overseas*
> *Sure brought Wales to their knees*
> *We'll say 'Da iawn' you must be chuffed*
> *You left us well and truly stuffed*
> *The Interception Blues*

It went down well in the packed pub though I think people were still too much in shock to truly appreciate it.

The great thing about doing shows like that was it got me greater recognition in the business. It proved to be the cross-over from 'Phil the rugby bloke' to 'Phil the all-rounder broadcaster and entertainer'. The world was my ostrich!

In 2001, I was asked to present a Sunday morning radio chat show called *Phil Steele's Big Easy*. I'd done a pilot which went well and then got offered a peak time show every Sunday on BBC Radio Wales. It brought me lots of work but, in retrospect, perhaps made me appear a 'jack of all trades, master of none'. Even today I get criticised by serious rugby followers for not being hardnosed rugby enough – for not going into enough detail – but that's not me. It's not my forte. Other people are much better at doing that. I'm me. I like to put my own spin on it. I like to keep it more light-hearted and try to emphasise the point that while rugby is a serious, professional sport, it also exists to provide enjoyment for its followers.

The broadcasting was really starting to take off and I

was given other presenting roles on all sorts of programmes including a summer series called *Steele Away*, in which I took part in many weird and wonderful lesser-known sporting events throughout Wales, such as a 5k race for naturists! Thank goodness it was radio!

During the 2000-01 academic year, I realised that the broadcasting and public speaking commitments were too much to handle whilst working full-time as a teacher, so I took the decision to reduce my teaching to a three-day week. Not because I'd had enough of teaching, but because my new career was blossoming and I wanted to give it space to grow.

8

To Be or Not To Be ... a Teacher

'The ability to entertain is a fabulous gift and being able to make an individual feel special when you speak to them is a very rare gift, yet Phil does these in all aspects of his life. He believes that these talents of his are commonplace – if only the rest of us had these commonplace gifts! The Ely Boy has done very well.'

Stuart Davis
Former teaching colleague and friend of 25 years

From 2001 to 2002 life seemed perfect. I was now working three days a week in school, my broadcasting and after-dinner speaking career had taken off in a big way and the Paroxatine tablets I'd been taking for a couple of years had made me stable. I was a new man!

Our lives were going so well, Liz and I decided to celebrate us both hitting 40 with a family trip around the world with Bryony, who by then had turned 14. We had a wonderful time and saw some amazing places in Singapore, Australia, New Zealand and Hawaii. We couldn't have been happier.

Whoever was dealing the cards for my 'life hand' must have

know how happy I was because the next card dealt was another dark and sad one.

In the summer of 2002, my younger sister Ann, who I'd been very close to when growing up, died of a drink-related illness. For many years she had been engaged to her long-term boyfriend from her school days but inexplicably, only weeks before their wedding, they abruptly split-up.

After that her life took a bizarre and eventually tragic course. Firstly, she met and quite hastily married a Moroccan chap named Ayashi, who was a tumbler in Gandey's Circus.

With him being a Muslim and Ann a Catholic, they compromised by holding the wedding ceremony in a registry office. Ann was by then a teacher in a Catholic primary school in Cardiff but the Catholic Church took a dim view of her not having the wedding service in a Catholic church, which was against Church Law. According to the Catholic authorities, she was deemed to be 'living in sin' and, as such, had broken her contract of employment, which stipulated that teachers were to do nothing in their private life that could be considered a 'bad example' and bring the Catholic faith into disrepute. As a result, Ann was made to resign her post. It caused quite a stir in the media at the time. I remember it was the lead item on the HTV evening news and the story was featured in several of the London-based daily papers. She was even interviewed on Channel 4's *Big Breakfast*.

I was livid. 'So much for Christianity,' I thought. I tried to get Ann to follow the advice of her union representative from the NUT, who told her not to resign but rather let herself be sacked so that they could vigorously fight her case on the grounds of unfair dismissal. She refused, and instead resigned with just three months' salary.

Looking back, all these years later, the fact that she didn't wish to fight for her job was probably a reflection of

Ann's deteriorating state of mind and the beginnings of her downwards spiral into a very dark place. I'd guessed that she'd started to drink heavily by then but I didn't appreciate just how much it had taken a grip on her. One day she asked me to go to the bank with her to act as a guarantor for a loan. She was very overdrawn but she needed cash. Another time, I lent her £100 because her husband needed new leather boots for his circus show. It wasn't the money that was the issue for me, it was the way her life was heading. A few weeks later, Liz and I went around to her house for dinner. Her husband, a quiet and pleasant man, suddenly got up from the table and disappeared. Ann said he'd gone upstairs to pray. I never ever saw him again. They split-up not long after and, looking back now, I think it might have been a marriage of convenience – just a means for him to get a British passport.

It became more and more difficult to have a relationship with Ann after that. I never really knew if she was telling the truth, even in day-to-day conversation, and as a result we lost touch. The next thing I heard, Ann had gone to Pakistan to teach for a Catholic missionary society. There she met a trainee priest, a Fijian named Tony. They must have fallen in love because he renounced the Church and they got married. Bizarrely, he went from training to be a servant of God to joining the British Army. They headed home to the UK and settled down in Oxford.

Ann did try and turn her life around, getting a job in a Catholic school in Kilburn, in London, but we still didn't speak. By then I didn't trust a word that came out of her mouth and, to tell the truth, I couldn't deal with the added stress. I didn't need someone else's problems to tip me over the edge and back into my own downward spiral.

Late one night, my brother John called to say that Ann was in hospital in Oxford. Allegedly, some kid in school had opened a door and she had walked into it. She had bruised ribs and internal bleeding. I thought it was an unlikely tale. I remember a book by Roddy Doyle called *The Woman Who Walked into Doors*, about a woman who didn't walk into doors! Ten days later, on a Sunday afternoon, John called again whilst I was getting things ready to go on my annual school camping trip to the Gower on the Monday morning.

"Ann is critically ill in intensive care," he said.

The worst thing about it all was, because I'd lost all trust in her, I didn't know if I should go to see he or not. That's a terrible thing to admit now, but that's how I felt. Also, I didn't want to let down my kids at the school – it was a 'once a year' experience for most of them – so I phoned the hospital to try and find out the exact situation for myself. Since I wasn't the next of kin, the nurse couldn't give me any details over the phone, but she did hint that if she were me and it was her sister, she'd go to her bedside immediately. Then I knew it was serious. I organised for another teacher to take the children on the trip and I drove up to the Radcliffe Infirmary in Oxford that night.

Ann lay in bed. She looked awful. Tony, who was a really nice guy, sat by her bed, holding her hand. She'd had a massive liver bleed. It was as if her liver had just exploded.

A nurse came in and asked us if we knew that Ann had a severe drink problem.

"Yes," I said.

Everyone else, including Tony, seemed shocked to hear the news. I still couldn't believe how people could bury their heads in the sand so deeply. Surely they couldn't have been that naïve!

Ann died that night.

When it was over, I was so glad I'd gone to see her. It took a while for me to appreciate that she had an illness just like me. I just couldn't see it at the time. She suffered, the same as I had suffered but in a different way. We both had our own way of dealing with it I guess.

Her death hit me hard. We'd been the closest in age and closest as far as getting on with each other when growing up. We liked each other's company until our lives and illnesses drove us apart.

The funeral service for Ann was held at our home parish church of St. Francis in Ely. Lots of Tony's Fijian friends and family came to pay their respects, which was lovely, and we buried her in a full Fijian burial shroud in the same grave as my mother and father. I stood there, by the graveside, feeling guilty. The worst thing was, that when my brother had phoned that night to say she was seriously ill, if I'm honest I'd say it was a phone call I'd been expecting. It was the call I'd known was going to come for the last ten years. It is a terrible thing to say that now, but it was true.

Could I have helped? Was there anything I, or we, could have done to make things better for her? Was the drinking her way of asking for help? Thoughts raced through my mind. It took a lot of soul-searching until, in the end, I concluded it had all been up to her. There was nothing I or anyone else could have done or said which would have made her stop. She was an addict. Only she could have made that decision and she needed to have come to that decision for herself. Every time she contacted me, she always seemed to want something but would never give anything back in return – and I don't mean the money. I just wanted her back the way she'd been – the talented and lovely individual I had known until she lost her battle. It was such a tragic end to her life at the age of 37. She was much too young to be taken away, and for what? A drink!

What a horrible, destructive disease any form of addiction is, be that drinking, drug taking, gambling or whatever. Now here I was, at 41, having lost both my parents and my closest sibling.

Even now, whenever I go out for a beer, after a few jars a little angel pops up on my shoulder and whispers, 'Hang on. Just be careful, you know what happened to your sister.'

It only takes a few pints to automatically trigger some sort of safety valve inside me; a safety valve which is there to protect me from ever going down that same road. The lifestyle I lead now in the media and public speaking can easily lead to a lifestyle of abuse in various forms. I've seen many individuals get pulled into the trap and never get back out. There are many temptations along the way. It's easy to have a drink at this function, one more at another event, followed by a couple of heavy nights when away covering a match and then another one at a dinner or two. It can soon build up.

In the midst of this family tragedy, my professional life was going from strength to strength. Working at the school just three days a week, gave me more time to do other things. My work at the BBC and after-dinner speaking opened more and more doors: Phil Steele the broadcaster and entertainer was now overtaking Phil Steele the teacher. It was as if people didn't regard me as a teacher anymore and I soon met more and more contacts from this new world. The invitations to speak at more diverse functions increased as did the fees they were willing to pay.

It was odd stepping outside the institutionalised world of teaching. You get ingrained in it. Starting at 9am with the bell, having set breaks and lunch times, terms and holidays.

Suddenly I was free, well, free-ish. I was still part-time but I was entering a new world. I had half climbed over that fence and I liked what I saw. I wanted more. It was great to know that people were willing to pay me money for my ability to entertain and for being me. It was a whole new ball game.

May 2007 was a watershed month for me. By now, my

school working days were Monday, Tuesday and Wednesday. One week I parked my car outside the school on the Wednesday morning because I didn't want to get blocked in by the school buses at home time. On hearing the bell I rushed out, like one of the excited school kids, and drove to Heathrow to catch the overnight flight to Qatar to speak at Doha RFC's club dinner on the Thursday night. When the dinner was over, I headed straight to the airport to catch the overnight flight back to Gatwick, followed by an early Friday morning bus to Heathrow to collect my car. Next, I drove to Cwmbrân to speak at a lunch for Croesyceiliog Cricket Club then hot-footed it to Blackwell RFC, near Weston-super-Mare, for their annual dinner, getting home at 2am. The next day I was off again, to speak at Kingsclear RFC in Hampshire, where I stayed overnight, before driving back to the BBC studios in Cardiff to do a voice-over for the *Scrum V* television programme on the Sunday afternoon. On Monday morning, bleary eyed and jet–lagged, I was back in school in Ystrad Mynach.

'This is going to kill me,' I thought. I had a massive wad of money in my pocket after four after-dinner events in three days, plus the BBC work but money was never the motivation for me. I needed to make a decision. I led this weird life. For three days of the week I worked in the Rhymney Valley in one of the poorest and most deprived areas in Europe, then when the bell sounded I would be flying first-class to Dubai or some other exotic location, staying at the best hotels and being treated like a rock star for four days, and then I'd be back in the Rhymney Valley on the Monday.

I liked the fact I was going back to school though. It kept me grounded. I think there was also the 'A' level in 'Guilt' kicking in again. 'You've been living it up for four days Steeley, now go back to do your penance, boy!'

I remember being in class one Monday morning, after flying

back from an after-dinner speaking gig at the Dubai Welsh Society's St. David's Day dinner, when one of my pupils asked if I'd had a nice weekend.

"Yes thank you Julie, I've been to Dubai."

Then, using classic Welsh valleys vernacular she replied "Ave ewe? whar dew buy?"

"No, Julie. Dubai."

Another kid piped up, "Yeah. But Sir, whar dew buy?"

"Sir's been shopping," another kid informed the rest of the class.

"No. I have been to Dubai."

"We know that Sir, but whar did ewe buy!!?"

If it had been a sit-com, it would have been pure comedy gold. I was dying to laugh, but didn't want to hurt their feelings.

After that manic weekend in May 2007, I made a life-changing decision. I decided that the coming September would be the start of my final school year as a teacher. It wasn't a decision I took lightly because, for most of my life, all I'd ever wanted to do was teach.

Liz backed me 100%. She knew it was time for a change and we both knew that if I didn't step away at that time, I never would. So, at the end of the summer term, in July 2008, I took the plunge and become an 'ex-teacher'.

By now I was nearer to 50 than 40 and not a young pup, a few years out of college, who'd got bored and was now looking for more excitement in his life. People didn't normally jump off the familiar work train at that age. Typically, they hung on to the side of that train for dear life, until they got their hands on their pension.

I was leaping off, to go and work in a very competitive and very fickle business. I wanted to go and swim in the shallow, shark-infested waters of the media, leaving behind the world of a caring, structured profession. I'd never been one to blow my own trumpet and I'm not really a pushy person, so it was a bit of a risk. Would I really be cut out for it? Although I lacked confidence and experience, I never lacked belief in what I could do. Deep down I knew I had the ability to give it a proper go.

From the start, I never once had the feeling that I didn't have the right skills. Looking back now, maybe I shouldn't have gone to college and become a teacher in the first place. Maybe I should have gone straight into the media or entertainment but hey, maybe if I hadn't gone down that route I may not have got to where I am today or even be the same kind of person. I've met people who I'd seen on TV for years and thought, 'Oh, she's nice' or 'he seems like a top bloke,' only to find out that one or two weren't like that at all. A few of them have been nothing but charlatans; full of their own egos and self-importance.

An honourable exception was my hero as a rugby commentator – the doyen himself – Bill McLaren. Like many rugby lovers of my age, Bill provided the soundtrack to the game through my childhood and beyond. It was then such as great thrill that I got to work with the great man on three occasions.

Bill had always reminded me of my father, in that they were virtually the same age and seemed cut from the same cloth – both dedicated to their work and absolute perfect gentlemen. When I first got to work with Bill, at a Pontypridd v Glasgow match at Sardis Road in 2000, he was exactly how I imagined him to be.

I was also privileged and honoured to interview Bill in the week leading up to his last international match commentary – on the Wales v Scotland Six Nations clash in Cardiff in 2002. He must have been in great demand for interviews that week but he was both generous with his time and gracious in his manner towards me. For my last question, I asked him how he would like to be remembered as a commentator and he simply replied, "I think Phil, just as someone who was fair and who appreciated good rugby no matter which team was playing it." I remember thinking then, what a great epitaph to a great career that was – and of course still is now that Bill is no longer with us.

After waving goodbye to my teaching career, I was now Phil Steele, the speaker and broadcaster, and nothing else. I knew I could do it and it felt wonderful. The best bit was this was me doing my stuff. It wasn't me teaching kids about someone else's stuff. I'd never felt happier. It was the most natural thing in the world. The thrill of knowing people were paying me, for being me, and for doing something I loved. Don't get me wrong, I loved teaching, but this was different altogether.

Around this time I didn't have one single depressive thought. Of course there was a natural concern about what could happen if it didn't work out, but there was no depression or its fiendish twin, the crippling anxiety. This was just a new adventure.

My first year out of teaching felt great. I was in greater demand, mainly as I had three extra days to offer and I could take bookings during the week and didn't have to be home early on a Sunday because of school the next day.

The transition was quick and painless, even in a cut-throat industry. I just tried to be myself. Of course I cared if someone said they didn't like my commentary or reports, or if they hadn't enjoyed my speech, but I was more concerned if they didn't think I was a good bloke. I tried to be nice to everyone I met. I'd always – and still do – make a point of saying hello to security guards, cleaners and workers in the canteen. The world of the media often doesn't lend itself to be like that. It's a world where he who shouts loudest – and is the rudest – goes the furthest. The pushier you are, the more you get on.

To celebrate my new career, in the first week of September

2008, instead of going back to school as normal, Liz and I went on a trip on the Heart of Wales railway line to Chester; my dad's love of rail travel is still strong in me. It was a wonderful feeling to sit on that train, eating cheese and crackers and sipping Chardonnay while wondering what my colleagues were doing back in school! It was a great feeling not having to get ready, with a knot in my stomach, on the Sunday evening before 'Black Monday – what many teacher's call the first day back for the start of a new school year.

Here I was, on a train with the woman I loved – totally relaxed – enjoying life and not bound by fixed school terms and holidays.

Just to rub it in, that January we went on a Caribbean cruise. It was perfect and also cheap. I'd always been confined to going away during school holidays, which were always the most expensive times. I felt like I'd 'made it', as we strolled through the airport without the mad rush of families all around us. This was the life. We talked about travelling around the world again and maybe following an Ashes cricket series or Lions rugby tour.

I was 47 and life couldn't get any better. It probably surpassed the time I'd spent in college, as the happiest I'd ever been. Bryony had done her 'A' Levels and had gone off to study Law at university in Norwich, Liz had enjoyed a promotion in work and was now a traffic engineer for Rhondda Cynon Taff council, we didn't have any financial worries and the anxiety had almost disappeared.

I felt like superman – indestructible. Nothing could puncture this feeling of happiness – could it?

Headphones and Headaches

'We are extremely proud to have Phil as one of our Ambassadors and he has given so much support to the charity over the past years. Being a skilled presenter and natural comedian he is always very popular, but it's his passion for the cause that is most noticeable. He doesn't do it to raise his profile, he does it because he really cares.'

Nicky Piper – George Thomas Hospice Care and former Commonwealth Light-Heavyweight Champion

One of the factors that helped me decide to give up teaching was that I'd taken on a new role for BBC Wales as the pitch-side reporter on the rugby programme *Scrum V Live* on Friday evenings.

This came about quite by chance and totally out of the blue. One Sunday morning in the autumn of 2005, I was enjoying a lie-in when I received an 8am phone call from Siôn Thomas, an executive producer at BBC Wales, telling me that due to unforeseen circumstances they were short of a pitch-side reporter for a live match that afternoon at Leeds between Yorkshire Carnegie and the Llanelli Scarlets. He asked if I could possibly get to the studios in Llandaff by 8.30am, to be picked up to travel north.

Like I said, the mindset of a freelancer is always to say 'yes' and then panic about the consequences later! So, at 2.30pm that afternoon, I found myself pitch-side at Headingley. It went well, thank God. The producer obviously liked what I had to offer and used me again in the role a few more times the following season.

I must have been doing something right, as in the summer of 2007 the producer of *Scrum V Live*, a top guy and great character named Huw Tal met me for a coffee and asked if I fancied taking on the role full-time. The former Wales international forward Stuart Davies, who had done the job previously, had other work commitments which prevented him from always being available and they were looking to use him more in a commentary and studio role.

I immediately rang Stuart, a great rugby man who has become a good friend, out of courtesy to tell him the news. I was relieved when he said he was delighted for me and that I should give it my best shot.

Suddenly, heading towards 50, here was I, about to be foisted on the Welsh viewing public every Friday night for 30 weeks a year with my headphones and microphone.

As normal, I wanted to try to do things a bit differently. The pitch-side reporter's job I felt should not just be about reporting facts and news about the game but rather to try to give the viewer a feel that they were 'part' of the match and not just merely spectators at home. I also wanted to try to reflect the fun, humour and banter that are part of watching a game live at the ground.

I tried other left-field things too. If I saw someone of interest in the ground, maybe a former international, someone from another sport, an actor, politician or even a parent of a player, I'd try to get a quick word with them on-air just to provide a brief diversion, particularly if there was a long break in play or the game had become a bit boring.

Probably my biggest innovation was getting to speak to coaches during the match. I'd often hear commentators say, 'I wonder what's going through the coach's mind at the moment?' So one evening, before a Cardiff Blues match, I asked their coach Dai Young if it would be ok for me to go up to him in the stand to get his thoughts for a few seconds during a break in play. Dai agreed.

The brief interview couldn't have gone better. It meant *Scrum V* had broken new ground in rugby coverage in this country – the 'in-match interview' with the coach. Other coaches such as Shaun Holley at the Ospreys, Paul Turner at the Dragons and Phil Davies of the Scarlets followed suit and it became a regular feature.

Nowadays most TV companies in the UK have it stipulated in their contracts that coaches must provide interviews during the game. When I started the trend it was by pure goodwill on the part of the coaches.

On a similar theme, I was the first reporter to do interviews with players who had been replaced on the field. I reckoned that getting a close-up shot and the view of a sweating, muddied, and bloodied forward who'd recently left the fray would give viewers a real feeling of authenticity and connection.

Of course, such access to players and coaches relies totally on trust and empathy and I'm always careful to pick my moments and questions carefully.

Being a former player helps with this inasmuch as I know first-hand how it feels to have had a good or bad game, a heavy defeat, or to have been on the wrong end of a dodgy refereeing decision! It sometimes feels like I'm an amateur psychologist having to read the mood and demeanour of my subject in a split second.

I like to think that all the players and coaches have sufficient respect and trust in me, as a rugby man, to know that I would never deliberately try to embarrass or demean them, or worse still, try to 'stitch them up'.

I understand that my style is not to everyone's taste, particularly with hard-core rugby fans, but I always try to make sure that nothing I contribute takes away from the importance of the action and the general narrative of the match itself. The game is the centrepiece but I try to get over to the viewer what it's like *at* the game as well as what's happening *in* the game.

Everything was going well and I was enjoying this new career and lifestyle but, it was when I'd just come back from working on a game for *Scrum V* in May 2009 that my life was to take another terrible turn.

I'd gone to Toronto for the Canada v Wales match and around the same time Liz had started complaining about having nasty headaches. At first I didn't think much of it. Ever since I'd known her, she had always suffered from tightness of the neck and shoulders. She put it down to the fact that she was a judo black belt and also played a lot of baseball.

Over the years she'd had a few operations to remove benign lumpy tissue from her breasts so obviously it was a concern, but we were told the three or four lumps were all scar tissue and that there was nothing to worry about. Of course I worried, but it made us both feel much better when, after each operation, she got the all-clear from the doctor. Since then she had been fine, looked well and had regular check-ups and various annual tests to make sure she stayed that way.

As the weeks went on, her heath didn't improve. In fact, her headaches got worse – they lasted longer and were a lot more severe – and her vision wasn't too clever either. She complained it was sometimes blurred but, Liz being Liz, she didn't let it affect her and she continued to go to work every day.

The Canada match at the end of May was an in-and-out assignment; flying out on the Thursday morning and back home on the Sunday. That week she didn't actually go to work because her headaches were so bad and she was being sick a lot. This was now really worrying me because it was so unlike her, but even though I made a strong argument not to go, she demanded I went.

"I'll be fine," she assured me. "Go!"

When I flew back a few days later, she was still no better. I wish I hadn't listened to her. I should have stayed. By now she was having difficulty sleeping and for two nights on the trot I took her to the out-of-hours GP unit at the Royal Glamorgan hospital. Both the doctors who examined her said it was a bad migraine and gave her tablets to relax the muscles in her neck. Nothing changed and the headaches were excruciating. On the Thursday I took her to her own GP, Doctor Angus McLean. His brother Ruarí had been in college with me so I knew him a little.

I pulled him to one side for a quiet word. "Angus," I said. I've never seen Liz like this in twenty-four years of marriage. I have never seen her in this much pain."

He examined her and I could immediately tell by his expression that he was concerned. He gave me a letter and told me to take Liz back to the Royal Glamorgan for a full check-up. I didn't wait, I took her straight there. She really was that bad. They carried out all kinds of tests; blood tests, reflex tests, every test under the sun. Surprisingly, they told us that everything seemed to be fine but they wanted to keep her there so they could take a scan, first thing the next morning.

I wanted to stay with her, but again she made me go home for a rest. I found it hard to sleep knowing she was lying there in hospital, so I was up early and just about to leave the house, to get back to Llantrisant, when the hospital called to say that

Liz had already undergone the scan and they wanted me to come in as soon as possible. The phone shook in my hand. I could sense instantly that this was going to be bad news. I rushed back to the hospital, where they ushered both of us in to see the consultant.

Without pulling any punches he came straight out with it. "We have found a large tumour in the frontal lobe of the brain." He said, looking at each of us in turn.

Even though I was sitting down, my legs turned to jelly. I gently squeezed Liz's hand as tears began to fill her eyes. I wanted to scream, but I couldn't even talk. The news was too hard to take in. Imagine how it must have been for Liz?

I wanted to tell the doctor that he must have made a mistake, but I could tell by his eyes he hadn't. How could this be happening to us? To Liz? We had just got the life both of us wanted and now our world had collapsed in just six words: "We have found a large tumour."

His words hit me as hard as if I'd been punched by Joe Calzaghe.

What I remember most was the silence in the room. No one knew what to say. Liz took my other hand in hers and tried to smile. I think she knew from the start that it was pretty bad. The doctor had just confirmed what she'd probably been thinking.

Then, without warning, the doctor threw us a lifeline. "But some better news," he added. "Because of its shape, which is very regular, there's a chance it could be a benign tumour."

A ray of light shone through the darkness. It was something to clutch onto. Even to me, a person who on many occasions had only ever seen the negative side of things, suddenly there was hope.

"She's going to be ok. It's only benign. It's only benign," I kept repeating to myself. For once I was the positive one – I guess I had to be, I had to be strong – but I also knew that hanging on to the fact it could be a benign tumour wasn't logical at all. It's ironic how I couldn't have been as positive at times like this in my own life. Why couldn't I have had a better outlook when things were going badly for me? The mind is such a powerful instrument and its strange how it can play tricks. Maybe it was because it wasn't me who was ill and therefore I was the one who had to put on the brave face.

Next, I had to drive to Cardiff to relay the news to Bryony, who'd just started a new job with a law firm in the city. That was such a hard thing to do. I'd had a quick chat about Liz with Bryony's boss before they called for her. Bryony burst out crying when she saw me. She had guessed something wasn't right.

"What's wrong Dad, what's wrong? Is it Mum?"

"Your mum's got a brain tumour," I said. I didn't know how else to explain it. I tried to comfort her but it was no use. I just held her tight while she cried.

For one of the first times in my life, I was trying to be the mentally strong one. For all the times I had fallen apart so easily in my life, now I needed to be brave. I needed my head to be screwed on. It was tough but I knew that I couldn't mentally crumple as I'd done in the past, like when I'd have a mini-breakdown just trying to kick a penalty for Newport. I had to be strong for Liz but how was I going to deal with the news that Liz had a brain tumour?

That night, I had a speaking engagement at a golf dinner in west Wales, with the annual dinner of Ammanford RFC booked for the following day. To be honest, I didn't feel I could do either and wanted to cancel both, yet Liz insisted that I be professional, so I very reluctantly agreed to keep the Saturday night booking in Ammanford but, for the first time in 25 years of public speaking I did withdraw from the event being held that night. I don't think I'd have been able to hold it all together, only hours after being told my wife had a brain tumour.

My great friend Richard Thomas drove me to Ammanford and I told the club chairman about the situation when I arrived. He was very understanding. The audience was fantastic and I'll always feel a special affection for Ammanford RFC because of their sheer warmth towards me on that night. It still felt so weird, making people laugh when in the back of my mind all this was going on. Outwardly, I must have appeared full of life, but inside I was slowly dying. I felt so guilty milking the applause when my wife, the love of my life, was so unwell.

The hospital had prescribed Liz with some strong steroids and painkillers, and early the next morning she called and sent a text with a list of items – clothes, food, make-up and other things – she wanted Bryony and I to take into the hospital with us. For the next fortnight she was almost back to her old self with boundless energy and feeling very little discomfort. Naïvely, for that brief period, I thought she was getting better and that she'd beat the illness.

However, even though the steroids helped her condition improve for a while, deep down I knew that this wasn't my Liz anymore. She looked like Liz but it wasn't really her any more. The more the tumour grew, the more functions in her body and mind were being lost and the more her personality changed.

I'll never forget taking her down from the ward to the shop on the ground floor of the Royal Glamorgan, where she wanted to buy a women's magazine. The doctors had told me not to do everything for her as it was important for her to feel independent. She went over to the counter with the magazine, which cost £1.75. She had about £2.20 in her hand, in loose change. The woman told her the price and Liz looked at the money in her palm. She stood there in silence for a while, just staring at her hand. Her mind couldn't register what she needed to do. It reminded me of when I used to teach the special needs children: giving them plastic money and watching them try to work things out, she couldn't process the information. She kept looking but couldn't work it out. In the end she looked up at the lady and said, "I'm sorry, please can you take the money for me."

It was heart-breaking. Here was my very intelligent, very talented wife – a judo black belt, a baseball player, and accomplished artist – who'd lost the ability to deal with notes and coins, a skill learnt by primary school pupils. I didn't know if I should laugh at the stupidity of it or wrap her up in my arms and hold her tight. It was awful and I knew it would only get worse.

After a week in hospital Liz came home and a week later the course of powerful steroids came to an end. She then returned to hospital for an operation at the end of June, the same time I was booked to speak at an educational conference dinner in Bedfordshire. Once again, I was determined not to go, but Liz said, "You have got to go. We can use the money to put towards our next holiday. I want us to go on another round the world trip."

As I left the hospital, floods of tears raced down my cheeks. I can feel myself welling up just writing this.

Off I went, over the bridge to my engagement, getting home at 3am for some rest before returning to the Royal Glamorgan to see Liz at 6am, prior to her operation at 9am. We were praying that the tumour would turn out to be benign and that the surgeon would be able to remove it. It was a forlorn hope. The operation merely turned out to be a biopsy. Due to its position in the brain the tumour couldn't be removed.

Worse was to follow when the surgeon told us that the tumour was a secondary cancer and that they didn't know where the primary tumour was.

All hope had drained away into a pit of despair.

Liz came out of hospital five days after the operation and was overjoyed to see all the cards, letters and flowers sent to the house by friends and family. I asked her what she'd like to do that evening.

"Take me down to Sam's," she said. "I think I fancy a curry."

Such a mundane request seemed wholly incongruous to the seriousness of the situation in which we found ourselves. I was grateful that at least it would provide a semblance of normality, if only for a couple of hours.

Samir, or Sam as he is known to everyone, is a lovely Bangladeshi guy who runs The Spice Connoisseur in Taff's Well, one of our favourite restaurants. As usual Sam gave us a great welcome and made a big fuss of Liz when we got there. She didn't look great, with a bandage on her head and she barely had any colour left in her face.

Sam bought over some poppadoms and the chutney tray but Liz had lost so much of her dexterity and motor control, she could hardly put her spoon into the chutney and soon she was spilling food all over the place. The more she tried, the worse it got. By the end of the main course it looked as if a small nuclear war had broken out directly over the table. There were quite a few other people in the restaurant, who started to stare. I began to feel stressed, wondering what they might be thinking.

I wanted her to be my normal Liz, the Liz I knew, the Liz of old, my lovely, beautiful and talented wife. Sam came over to our table and he didn't bat an eyelid. He cleaned up the mess with no fuss whatsoever, as if it was the most normal and natural thing in the world. He laughed and joked with Liz and he made us both feel completely at ease. He knew and understood the situation and was fantastic with us. It might seem trivial when reading this now but it was small acts of

168

kindness like that by Sam, and many others, that helped keep our spirits up during such a dark time. I'll always remember them.

It was amazing how everyone, relatives, friends, work colleagues and neighbours, rallied round to help. Lots of people called just to make sure that I was ok, that I was coping. Liz was the one who needed everyone around her but people knew I was struggling as well. Anyone would have struggled faced with that situation. I particularly remember several visits from Garin Jenkins, the ex-Wales hooker. Garin is an inspirational man who simply exudes humanity. No matter how stressed and worried I felt at the situation, a hour in Garin's company always left me uplifted and in better spirits – I'm sure Liz felt the same too.

The biggest stress came from the fact that I couldn't take my eyes off Liz for a second. She still wanted to try to do the normal things that by now had become impossible. She couldn't even make a cup of tea. It frustrated her. She loved the garden and loved watering the plants but even that became too much for her and I was afraid she would fall down the steps.

On the first Friday in July, we had the initial appointment at the Velindre cancer treatment centre in Whitchurch, Cardiff. The consultant sat us down, showed us Liz's brain scan and blurted out lots and lots of technical jargon. Then he got to his main point. "I will shrink the tumour by half with radiotherapy," he said calmly. "Definitely, and in the meantime if we find the primary tumour we can start you on a course of chemotherapy to attack that as well."

Was this hopeful news at last? No one had given us news like that since the early days. It felt at times as though everyone had given up. Now we had a saviour.

It wasn't all good news however, he told us that he couldn't start the radiotherapy for ten days because they had to mould a protective mask for Liz before they could start the treatment. He sounded more like a carpenter pricing up a job or a gas man coming to repair a leak than a doctor taking about cancer. 'I will service your boiler Mr. and Mrs. Steele, no problem.' He was so matter of fact, so clinical in his approach. Anyway, he'd given us hope and we were grateful for that.

Around the same time, we had a call from the nearby hospice to say that one of their nurses would be visiting Liz the following Thursday to check that she was comfortable, and that they'd do whatever else they could to help. That was fantastic news. There'd now be someone to help around the house, someone qualified to change her dressings, check her medication and, most importantly, someone I could talk to about the situation.

"We're going to beat this," I said to Liz, kissing her cheek as she fell asleep.

On the Monday, I asked Liz what she wanted to do. She asked to go on a day trip to Aberaeron, because her brother Adrian was sailing along the coast of Wales in his boat, and he was going to be there on that day. We drove up and had lunch in the Harbourmaster pub. Liz ordered Dover sole but had great difficulty holding her knife and fork. It's hard to eat Dover sole, with all the bones, at the best of times and in the end she abandoned the cutlery and resorted to using her fingers. It was another gut-wrenching episode for me to witness but Liz stayed brave.

On the same day we were in Aberaeron, news broke of the death of the great Welsh rugby captain, and ex-Taff's Well and Cardiff centre, Bleddyn Williams. On our way home we listened to a repeat of a programme, about his life and achievements, I'd made with him for BBC Radio Wales a few years previously. I was thinking how sad it was that he had passed away. Normally, Liz would have been chatty, telling me how she was enjoying the programme, asking me questions about Bleddyn's life and being generally engaging. But now, when I looked across at her in the passenger seat, she was sitting there, staring blankly out of the window. The pain I felt was almost physical – as if I'd been suddenly stabbed in the heart with a knife. I couldn't take my eyes off her. I wanted to pull over and hug her, to make her better. I wished it was me who had the tumour and not her. Men are supposed to be the ones to die first in a relationship. It wasn't supposed to be the other way around.

On the Tuesday evening, I went to play in a charity T20 cricket match for a Mike Gatting Invitation XI against Lisvane Cricket Club in Cardiff. I just needed to get out for a while or I'd have gone crazy. The Ashes were starting in the capital on the Wednesday and normally this would have been a massive deal for me. Even the thought of an Ashes Test being held in my home city would have been unthinkable when I was a sports mad kid growing up in Cardiff, but now I wouldn't have cared if it was to be played at the end of my garden. It had completely passed me by. Sport became irrelevant. The Lions were on tour in South Africa that summer but I'd barely even switched on the TV to watch a game.

On the Wednesday morning Liz asked me if I would take her to Ysgol Gyfun Rhydywaun, the Welsh-medium school in Aberdare where she had worked for a while as technician with her great friend Anne Marie Jones. They were the only non-Welsh speakers working at the school but there was no language barrier and Liz had really enjoyed her time there, making some great friends amongst the staff.

As we walked through the school yard, she grabbed onto my arm. "I'm going to fall, I'm going to fall," she said, as she slumped down and ended up sitting on the tarmac.

It was lunchtime and there were kids running and playing everywhere. One of them kindly came over and asked if there was anything he could do to help. He quickly dashed into the school building and a few minutes later came out with a wheelchair. Together we helped Liz up from the yard and placed her in the wheelchair. She was limp like a rag doll and could hardly support herself. How could my smart and wonderful wife be reduced to this? I wheeled her into the school office where all of her old colleagues made a big fuss, but she could hardly move her head to acknowledge them. When it was time to leave, Anne Marie came out to see us off. We managed to get Liz back into the car and Anne Marie hugged me. I knew from the hug that she knew how serious the situation had become. Few words were needed. "Take care now Phil, take care," she said softly.

Anne Marie told me a few weeks later that when Liz had got back into the car, she'd whispered a message to her, asking if she would 'keep an eye' on Bryony and myself, as she clearly knew her health was deteriorating fast; something Liz had never mentioned to me. Even though she must have realised she was dying, she'd bravely kept that realisation from her husband and daughter.

That night, she was in so much pain and vomiting violently that I phoned 999 for an ambulance. They took her to the Heath hospital in Cardiff and kept her in overnight. After staying with her for a few hours I drove the five miles back home to Taff's Well. The next morning, as I was leaving the house, the phone rang. It was the hospital calling to say that her condition had deteriorated. When I got there, she was in bed, semi-comatose. The consultant called me over to tell me she was very ill.

"We have a few options Mr. Steele," he said but I didn't really want to hear what they were. "If we don't intervene she will pass away in a few days, however, we could operate and put a shunt in the head to help the fluid drain and ease the pressure on her brain for a while."

"What will that do?" I asked.

"A shunt in her brain may extend her life by three months but I can't guarantee the quality of life."

Pardon the pun but it was a no-brainer. I knew she wouldn't want to suffer any more than she already had. "Don't put the shunt in," I replied.

He looked at me. "You are a very brave man," he said.

I wasn't brave. It was what Liz would have wanted. I didn't want to see her like that, and she wouldn't have wanted anyone to see her like that – especially Bryony.

On the Thursday night my great college friend Kevin Hopkins, the former Swansea and Wales centre, and his wife Gail, who is a GP, came to the hospital to see Liz. It was a very emotional couple of hours. We left the hospital at about 10.30pm, to go home for a few hours sleep, to give us the strength for what we thought would be a vigil for several days at Liz's bedside.

At a half-past midnight, the phone rang. I knew it was the herald of devastating news before I'd even picked up. Sure enough, it was the hospital.

"I'm sorry to have to tell you that Mrs. Steele passed away about five minutes ago," began a soothing female voice, "I also just want to let you know that your wife wasn't alone, one of the nurses was with her when she died."

"Ok. Thank you for letting me know," I replied.

Surprisingly, my overriding emotion at that moment was one of relief. Relief for the fact that Liz was no longer suffering and relief for me and Bryony that we no longer had to witness her suffering so badly. Of course I regretted the fact I wasn't there when she died, but I'm also convinced Liz didn't want us to endure the agony of watching her take her final breath, and somehow waited for us leave before passing away.

The date was 10 July 2009, almost a year since I'd given

up teaching. It had been precisely 35 days since her initial diagnosis. Now, at 48 years of age, I was a widower.

I still can't get over how kind people were. Wales' rugby legend and my BBC colleague, Jonathan Davies was one of the first to phone me. "I know how you're feeling Steeley. If there is anything I can do." He'd gone through the same thing a few years before when his wife had sadly been taken away by the same terrible disease.

We held the funeral at St. Teilo's RC Church in Cardiff, the same church where Bryony had been baptized 22 years previously. In a strange quirk of fate, it was Father Eddie O' Connell, the priest who had married Liz and I in St. Francis 24 years before and was now the parish priest at St. Teilo's, who conducted the service.

It was one the biggest funerals the church had ever seen with well over 500 friends, family and acquaintances coming to pay their last respects. The church was so full that many mourners had to stand and the coffin could barely make it down the aisle.

Liz was carried into the church to the song *You're My Best Friend* by the American country singer Don Williams, which had also been the theme tune we'd used in our wedding video. At my request, no one wore black so the church radiated with masses of bright colours, as befitting the celebration of a great life.

Liz's brother Adrian gave a superb eulogy, which was both poignant and humorous. My BBC colleague Frank Hennessy, and his musical partner Dave Burns sang during the service, before Liz's coffin was finally carried out, to the Queen song *These Are the Days of Our Lives*. She was a big fan of the band.

During the wake at Taff's Well RFC another great friend, the brilliant comedian Rod Woodward, did a turn as his alter ego, Mario De Nero.

HEADPHONES AND HEADACHES

At the end of the wake people came up to me and said, 'I know I shouldn't say this but I enjoyed that funeral.'

I was so pleased because Liz would have loved it. I felt similar emotions at the funeral to those I'd experienced at our wedding and, in a strange way, it was one of the proudest days of my life. It was fantastic to see all those people there for her, remembering her and celebrating her life. She was such a popular person.

Looking back now on the whole episode of Liz's illness and death, my overall feeling is one of total bewilderment. Everything happened so quickly. One minute I was living the dream and enjoying the perfect life, yet within a few weeks I was a widower. It was almost like watching someone else's life being acted out in a movie.

Even now, seven years on, there are many unanswered questions. I wonder if and when Liz knew that her illness was so serious, could we have done something different? Could the doctors have acted differently?

In lieu of flowers at the funeral, £4,500 was raised from donations for the hospice and, as a result, they asked me to become an ambassador for the charity. I accepted and now do quite a bit for them. Similarly, I'm often asked to speak at and host events for Velindre cancer hospital. They are fantastic charities which do great work but the great irony is, that in Liz's hour of need, her illness progressed with such speed that she was unable to benefit from either.

A few weeks later, on a brilliantly sunny, early autumn morning, we scattered Liz's ashes into the sea off The Point at Little Haven in Pembrokeshire, which was one of Liz's favourite places on this earth and where we had enjoyed our first holiday together 26 years earlier.

Little did I realise then how big a part Pembrokeshire was to play in my future life.

10

Team Kate

'Phil Steele embodies all that is great about the culture of Welsh
rugby. From grass roots to the elite, he approaches the game
with passion, humour and insight. Whether he's on the touchline
or the rugby club stage, he brings his trademark wit and warmth
and is much-loved and respected on the Welsh rugby circuit. Phil's
strength of character and sense of fun are all the more impressive
given some of the dark and devastating times he has endured.
His candour in discussing his experience of depression has given
others the courage to do the same and helped remove the
stigma of an issue that touches so many people. I am proud and
privileged to call him a friend.'

Carolyn Hitt
Writer and Broadcaster

Being without the woman I loved more than anyone else in
the world seemed just too hard to imagine. It is hard to even
start to describe in words how tough it was. As well as missing
the obvious little things, one of the biggest things I missed was
the lack of activity and noise in the house when I came home
from work. The absence of animation, which is the difference
between a living in a house and a home.

When Liz was alive, I used to look forward to coming home

after a long day at work. Walking through the door to hear the sound of the TV on in the lounge or the waft of cooking from the kitchen teasing my nostrils, accompanied by the percussion of pots and pans. Although Liz's cooking was great she couldn't help being noisy and she always seemed to make a giant mess when preparing dinner. There would be pots and pans and plates and spoons and dishes covering every inch of workspace. I'd always teased her about it. I was the opposite. I'd always put things away as I went along. I liked a tidy kitchen. She teased me about that!

Now all of our gentle banter had disappeared. When I entered my house, the only sound there to greet me was the sound of silence. All life had been taken away, lost through the bricks and mortar. I would have given anything to have walked into the kitchen and the place to have been in a right mess. Just to have seen all the dishes piled up everywhere and Liz gently chiding me as I began to help tidy them up. But there was no noise, no cooking smells and no messy kitchen. There was nothing.

Coming home proved to be just another reminder of what I had lost. A stabbing pain shot straight through my heart every time I entered that empty, cold house. The lack of noise, the lack of love, the lack of that woman's touch, my Liz's touch.

I would switch on the TV just to create the sound of life in the house. Sometimes when I made a cup of tea, I'd forget and automatically pull out two mugs.

I didn't know if I'd ever get over it. The nights lying in bed were even worse. You get used to lying next to someone. Used to someone's ways.

I never, for one moment, thought I would ever be without Liz. Even as we grew older together, I'd always imagined it would be me, the man, who would die first. It would be Liz crying at my funeral, remembering some of the weird little quirks I had.

As the weeks turned to months and the darkness of the winter nights approached, after work I'd go home and close the door on the world. The nights were long and the silence became more painful. In the past, I'd come home from a speaking gig and I'd be buzzing – my entire body pumped full of adrenaline. Whatever the time, I'd pop my head into the bedroom, where Liz would be half-asleep and I'd say, "The legend's home!"

"Hello Legend, how did it go?" She'd murmur.

Excitedly I'd tell her all about it. What went well and who was there. It didn't matter if it was two in the morning, she would be there, listening. I loved telling her all the details and she would let me talk and talk until I'd run out of things to say. Then she would roll over and go back to sleep. I'd kiss her goodnight and *cwtch* up next to her. What could be more perfect than that?

It's really strange how doing one of the most basic, regular little things in life can bring you back to reality with a bang. A few weeks after her death, for the first time in my life, I found myself filling in a form and ticking the box marked 'widower'.

It felt so bizarre not ticking the box which said 'married'. I stared at the word written in the box for a full ten minutes – my brain refusing to register it. It wouldn't sink in. It was as if my mind was fighting against it. It was trying it's best to put my head into a tailspin. Times like that left me in no man's land with no escape on the horizon.

Thankfully, although I was going through the normal grieving process during that period, the same as anyone else would, I didn't have clinical depression. I never once had the anxiety or the sense of darkness which I'd had in the past but I did increase my medication slightly, mainly just to reassure myself that I wouldn't slip down that slope again.

I sensed that there were more than a few people who feared that I might fall back into another episode of depression. That

I was going to lock myself away in my own little world but it wasn't like that at all. I had responsibilities. I had Bryony to look after and to try to help her get through our loss. To be fair, although she was still young we both helped each other. We cried together, we sat in silence and held hands together, we even laughed at the great memories we had as a family together. She helped me as much as I helped her.

I also had my friends and family who kept me sane at that time. The boys involved with the *Scrum V* programme deserve a special mention. As the nights drew in, the start of the rugby season proved to be a saviour for me. Alone in the house on a Monday night, my only saving grace was looking in the diary and thinking, 'Good. We're going to Edinburgh, Dublin (or wherever) to cover a game on Friday.'

The fact that I knew I would be enjoying a few days away, concentrating on something else and having a few beers and a *craic* with the boys, helped me enormously.

Their friendship provided massive support. People like Gareth Gronow, Joe Towns, Ross Harries, Huw Tal, Rhys Edwards, Craig Whithycombe, Gareth Charles, Stuart Davies, Brian Morrell, Rick O'Shea, Rhydian John and Dickie 'Bach' Jones became almost like a surrogate family. Even today, there is still a very special bond between us. Our time together was much more than us merely doing our job as colleagues. They knew what I was going through and they were just what I needed. My former teaching colleague, Stuart Davis, himself a widower, was also a great source of help and strength.

Being alone in the house was hard, yet going out was often much worse. As the months rolled on, I got invited to various parties and functions. It was like going back in time to when I was a single bloke, but by now there weren't many other unattached people at these events, as everyone else appeared to be with their spouses or partners. Often they'd be couples that Liz and I used to meet up with and talk to at such events.

Now it was me. Me on my own. There can be few sadder things in life than the feeling of being lonely in a crowded room. It was pure purgatory standing there, trying my best to hold onto a smile while hoping to blend in. Often it didn't work. Concerned people would come up and tell me how sorry they were for my loss, how Liz was one in a million and other touching, truly heartfelt sentiments. It was lovely to hear but it tore at my heart strings. On more than one occasion the emotion got too much and I had to leave.

I also focused quite a bit of my attention and time fundraising for various charities, especially those concerned with cancer. I arranged and hosted a gala sports dinner in memory of Liz, in aid of the hospice, and the support I received from family, friends and especially the sporting fraternity, was absolutely overwhelming. Even Wales coach Warren Gatland came along for the whole evening despite the fact that it was less than 48 hours before Wales were due to play against South Africa. The night proved to be a great success and raised over £12,000 for the charity.

This will sound strange, but it got to the point where I almost became some sort of professional widower. I was in the public eye, so it did feel like I was getting rolled out to not just comfort people who'd been through a similar thing but also, I assumed, because I could help raise the profile of the charity and maybe raise more money. I didn't mind that. It's a privilege to be able to do it. I'm proud to say that now, seven years on from Liz's death, I still do quite a bit for various cancer charities.

I remember one night, maybe about nine months after Liz's funeral, I was asked to speak at a black tie function in Fagins, my local pub in Taffs Well, in aid of the Lymphoma Association charity.

It didn't finish until the early hours of the next morning and I found myself walking, or slightly staggering, home about 5 am. It had been one of those nights when I lived up to the motto I first learnt during my student days, that you 'never come back in on the same day you go out'. It hadn't been planned that way of course, which often makes for the best nights out.

As I walked across the bridge over the A470 towards my house, the sun was coming up. I stopped and looked down at the road below me. Although it was early there was still a steady flow of heavy good lorries driving at full speed underneath. A fleeting thought crossed my mind: 'If I jumped off the bridge now, I'd be with Liz.' The thought just came to me. It wasn't like the suicidal thoughts I'd had before, they seemed quite logical at the time. This wasn't despair; it was quite matter of fact really. Maybe most widowers would think the same way. It could have been totally natural. I stared down at the road beneath me, then I thought of Bryony and what she meant to me. I cleared the thoughts from my head and carried on walking home, wondering why life was so unfair.

As the weeks rolled into months, the fear of being on my own was scary. I began to notice older people wandering around on their own in the town. They always looked so sad. I wondered would that be me? Was I destined to be one of those people? People need people. I needed Liz.

Bryony had now come back to live at home which was some consolation. She had graduated with a degree in Law from the University of East Anglia the year before and was now working as a legal executive for a Cardiff law firm, prior to her taking a yearlong LPC (Legal Practice Course) at Cardiff University. It was the final step she needed to take in order to fulfil her ambition of becoming a solicitor.

As the mist of Liz's death began to clear, or get less foggy, reluctantly I found myself in the new, big, wide world. A world I hadn't seen or been near for over 25 years – that of a single man looking for female company. I knew I had to move on, and with Bryony's blessing I tried.

It proved a strange thing to do. I couldn't believe how much the dating game had changed since I'd met Liz when I was twenty-one. Saying that, from the very beginning, I'd never really been one of those people at the front of the queue in the dating game and, what made it worse, I was now in that 40-60 bracket where people were coming out of broken relationships or, like me, had lost a partner. It was a different world and, if I'm honest, a bit of a free-for-all. It was a real eye-opener.

So with my eyes wide open, I got back on the old hamster wheel known as courting. I had a couple of relationships and the odd fling but they didn't work out. I'm not saying the women were at fault at all, far from it. I did try but things never felt quite right. Maybe it was too early. Maybe Ms. Right hadn't come along yet. Maybe Ms. Right would never and could never come along.

That all changed in December 2011. It was the Wednesday before Christmas and I went out 'on the town' in Cardiff with two of my old college mates, Gareth Francis and Marc Batten, who had both become Assistant Head Teachers in their respective schools. The boys had been fantastic since I'd been widowed, always making sure we met up for a couple of pints during every school holiday and half-term break.

As usual at that time of year, the city centre was buzzing with lots of people from office parties wandering from pub to pub. I couldn't really be bothered to join in the festive celebrations. I felt shattered and was looking forward to going for pie and chips in Cardiff's famous Caroline Street and then heading home. For some strange reason, after visiting 'Chip Alley' we decided, since it was Christmas, we should go to the pub for a last pint.

Whilst standing at the bar, I noticed two ladies over in the corner. One was blonde and the other had short black hair and the most dazzling smile I think I'd ever seen. After a while, the blonde girl came bounding over and said, "Oh, it's Phil! Hi Phil, I haven't seen you for ages." I was taken aback as I didn't recognise her at all. I tried really hard to recall how she knew me, but nothing registered. "I'm Helen," she said. "I'm a great friend of Suzanne's daughter Vicky."

The penny slowly dropped. In her spare time Liz had also run a small garden design business with a friend called Suzanne, who had a daughter called Vicky.

I remembered then that Liz and I had been to Vicky's wedding a few years back and that we had actually sat on the same table as Helen. After some small talk I sheepishly asked, "Hey Helen, who's your friend? And does she ever stop smiling?"

"That's Kate," she replied. "She's amazing, come over and meet her."

I looked across and smiled again. She beamed back again. She was so pretty and her smile was mesmerising.

"Come on, come and meet her," Helen insisted.

I gave myself a quick internal pep talk, something along the lines of 'You'll need to be punching above your weight again here Steeley!'

Helen introduced us. Kate's smile was even better close-up. She had no idea who I was, which immediately made me feel more relaxed as our conversation started.

"Where are you from, Kate?" I asked.

"I live in Pencoed," she replied, "but I'm originally from Pembrokeshire."

Now I don't know, in heaven's name, where my reply came from and I wouldn't really recommend anyone using it as a chat-up line, but I blurted out, "Oh, Pembrokeshire, my late wife's ashes are scattered off The Point at Little Haven in Pembrokeshire!"

Kate kept smiling but there was a brief silence before I nervously tried to explain what I meant. I'd ruled myself out of any prize in the 'Chat-up Line of the Year' awards but at least I'd subconsciously got the message over, without any messing, that I was single and a widower! Maybe Kate thought it was a bit of a joke but for once that wasn't my intention. It was just me being open and honest.

However, it did break the ice. We chatted away about Pembrokeshire for what seemed like ages and then about Pencoed. I asked Kate if she knew my best mate Kevin Hopkins and his wife Gail, who was a doctor in the village. It turned out Gail was actually Kate's GP. That was another link between us and another reason to carry on with our conversation.

On leaving the bar that night, Kate gave me her mobile number and told me that I could call her anytime. On the Friday, Kevin and Gail had organised a bit of a Christmas meal and party for their friends and neighbours in Laleston, near Bridgend, where they live. I'd already brought two tickets for the night at the Great House hotel in the village, one for me and one for another lady I was going to take, but by then our brief relationship had ended. Gail said they wanted to make the evening a bit different and had asked me to say a few words, for 20 minutes or so, after the dinner and before the disco.

Never one to shy away from an opportunity, I agreed and also said that I'd bring the guitar and sing a Christmas song as well.

I wanted to ask Kate if she fancied going with me but being rather old-fashioned, I sent her a text on the Thursday to ask if she minded if I called her. I didn't think it was right just to call her on the off chance.

'Of course,' came back her reply.

I rang and asked if she would be free the next day, the Friday and would she like to come to dinner at the Great House.

"Yes that will be lovely," she replied. I was sure I could hear the excitement in her voice.

"Err...just to let you know that there's not only going to be the two of us," I slowly muttered.

"Oh ok, how many are going to be there?"

"About 48!" I laughed, seeing the funny side of our first date being with a large crowd of other people, and there was more to come. "Oh, there's one more thing"

"What's that?"

"After the dinner, you'll see me get up from the table, speak to everyone for 20 minutes then pick up my guitar and sing the Shane MacGowan song, *Fairy Tale of New York*."

I wasn't purposely trying to impress her. I was just trying to lower her expectations for the night.

Without batting an eyelid, she replied, "Great...that's my favourite Christmas song!"

'That's not a bad start,' I thought to myself.

Even though we shared a crowded room, it was a truly wonderful first date and we soon got to see each other more and more. In early January I took her home to Bryony – a big step in any widower's relationship.

Out of respect, Kate didn't actually want to go into the house but waited on the driveway for Bryony to come out and say hello. Bryony appeared and the rest, as they say, is history. They talked for ages and I could see instantly that Bryony liked her. 'Yes!!' I thought, with an inward fist pump.

After taking Kate home and returning back through my front door, I found my daughter in the kitchen making tea. I said straight out, "What do you think of Kate?"

Excitedly, Bryony almost shouted back her immediate reply, "Dad, don't mess this one up whatever you do."

That was the sign I needed. A sign that Kate was the one. I knew within a couple of weeks that she was, in every way, in a different league to anyone else I had met since Liz had died. Everything just clicked between us. The way it all panned out with Kate being friends with the daughter of one of Liz's best friends seemed to me as if it was fate. It was almost as if Liz had let me try to find someone myself and had then stepped-in saying, 'You've tried your best and it's obvious you haven't found the right woman yet, so I'll help you – here she is!!!'

We never looked back and got engaged in September 2012 then married in April 2013, with my great friend Kevin Hopkins as our best man. The service was held at St. Mary's RC church in Bridgend, the parish in which I'd been a teacher 23 years earlier. The service was conducted by my old friend and former St. Joseph's (Cardiff) RFC prop forward, Father Tim McGrath, who is a great character and, like he had done at Liz's funeral, Rod Woodward had everyone in stitches with another brilliant comedy performance at the reception. All in all it was an unforgettable day with an amazing feeling of goodwill and happiness.

A few weeks later, for our honeymoon, we went out to Australia to follow the Lions rugby tour. I know, I know, you can call me an old romantic, but Kate loves rugby. I'm all heart!

I'm so fortunate that Kate and Bryony have such a great relationship. They've had it from day one. Bryony will now text or phone Kate before me and, to be honest, I really love that. "I'm Team Kate, Dad," she always reminds me.

Bryony's now qualified as a solicitor, having fulfilled an ambition that's she's had since she was 14 and her mum would be so proud of her for that. Kate is chief executive of SHINE, the charity which supports people with Spina Bifida and Hydrocephalus and she frequently ropes me in to do things for that very worthwhile cause.

To add to my delight, I now have another family with two beautiful grown up stepdaughters, Hanna and Louisa, a lovely sister-in-law in Emma and two nieces, Olivia and Anya, together with a nephew, Harry who is a promising wheelchair basketballer and athlete.

Harry, who is sixteen, has Spina Bifida and it's been a really humbling experience to see how he copes day-to-day with what is a severe disability. He is a constant source of inspiration and a reminder to me that even though I have had my difficulties, other people have to face their own daily struggles.

I'm still very close to Liz's mum Judith, who I actually still call 'Mum', and of course I also now have a second mother-in-law, Kate's mother Anne who is great fun and a real Pembrokeshire 'character'.

I wonder what bad deeds I must have done in my life to deserve to have two mothers-in-law?!!!!!!

But seriously, as far as my family life is concerned, I must be the most contented man in the entire world.

11

Blowing the Whistle on Depression

'Phil Steele is one of God's angels'

Dr. Clive Norling
Former International Referee

The most important reason why I wanted to write this book was to see if my story would in any way help other individuals who are also suffering from this terrible illness. To give them hope that all is not lost and that they can get through it and come out the other end intact.

When I was really bad the first time around, one of the primary feelings I had was that I was never going to get better. People suffering from depression often describe not being able to see the light at the end of the tunnel. At my worst, there didn't even seem to be a tunnel to walk through, never mind me trying to see the light at the end of it. Like lots of sufferers I couldn't picture any hope, any future or any escape at all.

I didn't think I would experience pleasure again in whatever form that would take. The simple joys of life, like watching a television programme or reading a good book, had deserted me. Even the simple pleasure of walking into a familiar and favourite restaurant or bar became an ordeal, as I'd be constantly feeling that everyone was staring at me and

188

whispering behind my back: judging me. Life abruptly became a place of darkness, with specs of grey. I was colour blind to the beauty and wonder of the world.

One of the worst feelings was the fact that I couldn't, or didn't want to, plan for anything. On more than one occasion, I couldn't see myself getting to tea-time, never mind what my life would be like in two years' time.

It was that awful feeling that I was always going to be ill. Not like when someone has the flu, when you know you just need to ride it out because, in a few days' time, you're going to feel better. In two days you know you'll be sitting up in bed watching some crappy afternoon TV show while tucking into a bowl of tomato soup. That's when you know you are on the mend. Depression isn't like that at all. I couldn't see any way out. I felt as if I was stuck in a circular building with no doors or windows or fire escapes.

I used to sit in my parent's house, repeating to myself, "If only I could see myself improving. If only I could see myself improving."

My mother would pipe up, "You are improving. You have improved."

The key was that I didn't feel like I was improving. There were times when I felt as if I was one small step away from being cast out into the darkness forever. When I started to get suicidal thoughts, because I couldn't face life like that anymore, it became a massive vicious circle. I did try and fight back on occasions. I'd get up in the morning and think, 'Yeah this is it; I'm going to be better.'

It never worked. I always felt worse, which just piled more misery onto my seemingly perpetual unhappiness.

The cruel thing about depression is you don't get better in a straight line. You get slightly better then, for whatever reason, you go backwards or downwards, or both. There was never a simple upward trend with me. It was up and down, up and down with often more downs than there were ups. One step forward and two steps back. I would drop back, the 'blip' they call it, where I felt ten times worse. I didn't know then but by the end of that first nasty bout, at least the graph was going in the right direction.

My mother was especially strong for me. "Phillip," she once said – she always called me Philip, if I did something wrong or she had an important point to make – "Not only will you get better, but someone will come to you later on in your life and you will be able to help them. You will be there to help and aid others. Don't ever forget that...."

Fast forward 23 years to July 2007, and I was speaking at a dinner for Bonymaen RFC in Swansea. Afterwards I had a chat with an ex-rugby referee Ken Parfitt and the name of Clive Norling came up. Most rugby folk people will remember Clive as, without doubt, the best and definitely the most flamboyant rugby referee of his generation and a genuine star of the game who revolutionised refereeing. He was a master of his craft, a brilliant communicator and confidence personified.

In a hushed tone, Ken whispered, "You haven't heard have you? He's very ill. He's got depression." I always find it amusing when people talk in hushed tones when telling someone about someone else who has depression, or cancer or another serious illness, as if the illness is going to accidentally hear you and get angry!

Normally, the response when someone hears bad news like that is the recipient usually replies in an even quieter hushed tone. But not me. Without hesitation I boldly replied, "Has he? I've had that too. Have you got his number please?"

At first Ken looked at me as if I was a little crazy, but I had long gone past the point of no return in caring about what people thought about my illness. In my mind I was already looking to find the nearest phone box to run into and appear, seconds later, with my pants outside my trousers – *Super Steeley, ready to rid the world of the evil Doctor Depression and his trusty sidekick, Anxiety!* – Ken duly gave me Clive's number.

I was now a man on a mission. A man with my mother's words of encouragement ringing in my ears.

That chat with Ken was on a Saturday night. On the Sunday morning I was doing a sports bulletin shift for Radio Wales and, during a break, I called Clive's number. Mair, his wife – or his 'better half' as he calls her – answered.

Calmly and gently I said, "Hello, I'm Phil Steele. I'm a former rugby player and I now work for the BBC. I know Clive and I've heard that he's not very well, that he's suffering from a nasty bout of depression." I could somehow tell from Mair's silence that this was a phone call with a difference. "Just to let you know," I continued, "I've had depression as well. I'm on medication, which I take every day of my life. I'm ok now and if Clive would like to talk to me, or if there's any way I could help, just let me know."

"Hang on Phil," she said. I could hear her walking away.

I didn't realise it at that time but he wasn't taking phone calls from anyone and he wasn't seeing visitors either.

"Yes," her voice whispered down the phone a few moments later. "Yes, he would like you to come and see him, as soon as possible."

At the other end of the phone I smiled to myself. Mair says, even to this day, that she doesn't know how or why Clive agreed to me visiting him, but she was so glad that he did.

A few days later, I found myself pulling up outside their house in Birchgrove near Swansea. I had no idea what I was going to say when I went in and I didn't have a script prepared in my mind. I just knew and believed that I could help him in some way.

The awful thing about depression is that it robs you of your own being. Its strips you of your confidence and leaves you feeling exposed and scared. This is exactly the scene that I found when I walked into the house. Clive was sitting in a chair in the corner of the room. This once great, confident, giant personality of Welsh rugby – a bigger star in his day than most of the players – was hunched with a handkerchief scrunched to his face, sobbing. He looked terrible. He looked frightened, grey and gaunt.

I began to talk to him. Trying to tell him how I had the illness, how it had made me feel, how I had been exactly like he was but, crucially, that I'd eventually dealt with it.

"I can't see the future Phil, I can't see the future," he kept repeating. "I can't read a newspaper or a book. I can't concentrate I have no interest in anything anymore." Tears rolled down his cheeks.

It was like looking at myself in the mirror back in 1984. It was me, sitting there in his chair. Me, sitting there feeling frightened and disconnected. Me, feeling alone, on a boat to nowhere, with wave upon wave of anxiety and gloom crashing over me, knocking me over every time I tried to get to my feet.

I took Clive's hand and didn't let go. Just talking to him made me realise how bloody evil depression can be, how sly it is and how it doesn't care about anyone or anything. It purposely goes out of its way to make you believe that you are nothing, a nobody, useless, hopeless and that you will never ever be your normal self again.

I stayed there all afternoon and when I left, I looked him in the eye and said, "You will get better Clive, I promise you. Just stick with it, hang on in there. Keep on with your treatment and medication and you'll get there."

It looked like he was trying to agree, but I don't think he truly believed me. At that early stage of his illness I don't think he was capable of believing me. I spoke to Clive and Mair on the phone every week and went to visit him every few weeks. Mostly, I just tried to provide reassurance, which I was able to do by informing Clive that the symptoms he had were exactly the same as I had suffered too and crucially, that he wasn't alone.

As I left his house one time, when he was having a particularly bad day, I remember saying to him, "Clive, not only will you get better, but when you are well, you and I are going to record a radio programme about this illness as a way of helping other sufferers."

He nodded in agreement.

Time is the friend of the depressive and slowly but surely, over the months, Clive's condition improved. He started to look better and talk more, especially about rugby and he even smiled and laughed. I remember one day he came out with one of his old trademark, dry-witted, mickey-taking quips at my expense. I was delighted because it was a sign that he was getting back to his old self.

I remember winking and saying to Mair, "Norling's back!"

True to my word, in April 2009 as Clive's recovery gathered pace, we recorded a two-part programme for BBC Radio Wales documenting his battle with the illness. *Clive Norling – Whistling in the Dark* was broadcast during Depression Awareness Week and received considerable critical acclaim, being nominated for both the Mind Mental Health Media Awards and the Celtic Media Awards.

It's my belief that humour can be found in almost any situation if you're attuned to it, even a programme on depression. My producer for the programme was a great guy named Steve Groves. Not only is he a superb producer but he's also suffered from depression. We recorded the programme in Clive's house and, after introducing Steve to Clive and Mair, she went into the kitchen to make us some tea, leaving us three men alone in the sitting room.

"Steve is one of us as well," I said to Clive, trying my best to break the ice and to get Clive feeling as comfortable as possible. "He's suffered from depression."

"Oh," said Clive. "what do you take for it Steve?"

"Citolopram," replied Steve obligingly.

"Interesting, and how much do you take?"

"I take 20 milligrams," said Steve.

"Only 20? I take 40," replied Clive.

"Ah, but I've taken Prozac as well – 40mg," Steve batted back.

It was my turn to interject. "Well, I had my last bad bout 12 years ago and I still take 10mg of Paroxetine every day!" I said, trying to outdo them both.

"10mg? Only 10mg? Call yourself depressed?" they replied, almost in unison.

This supposedly serious conversation about anti-depressant medication had suddenly descended into a Welsh version of Monty Python's famous *Four Yorkshiremen* sketch where four businessmen try to outdo each other in explaining how poor they once were.

I was half expecting the line, "I was so depressed, I spent three months living in a brown paper bag in a septic tank!" to come out!

We all realised roughly at the same time the bizarreness of the situation and we were laughing like fools when Mair entered with the tea and *bara brith*. She looked at us as if we were balancing on the edge of craziness.

Thankfully, Clive is now fully recovered and does a great job in helping to provide awareness of mental illness by talking freely about his experiences in press and media interviews and on other platforms. He's back as a hugely enthusiastic watcher and supporter of rugby and has also completed a PhD in Business – a course he had to put on hold during his illness – so he's no longer 'Ref' but Dr. Norling – as he never fails to remind me!

Now, if someone mentions to me that they are suffering from depression, I always say straight out and upfront, "I take Paroxetine...what do you take?" It always seems to be the key that opens up the door to let me in to help.

Wherever I go I meet people with depression or who have suffered from it at some stage in their lives. There are lots of sportsmen and women who suffer. To be truthful, I could pick a full Welsh rugby team of ex-internationals who I know have had experience of the illness.

I don't purposely go out of my way to push it down people's throats but I believe I can and do help people. They seem to gravitate towards me. I must be giving some sort of vibe. I'm quite open about it and I'm definitely not ashamed of what I've been through. I just want to help people. If I hadn't found help, I may not have been here now. Worryingly, the current suicide rate among men in the 45-59 age bracket is the highest it's been in 35 years.

Half the battle is knowing that you are not alone. Knowing others are going through it or, better still, have gone through it and have come out on the other side, a better person.

It is strange because depression doesn't care for class, race, intelligence, wealth, education or age. It can strike anyone at any time from any walk of life. It can strike with such a force, that you don't know what's hit you or why.

Hopefully, I've got my life sorted. I have a great job, I travel the world and I have another lovely wife and family. I consider myself very fortunate. However, that doesn't mean anything when it comes to depression, as it can strike anyone at any time. Many famous people have had it, successful people you'd never have imagined suffering from depression, like Charles Darwin, Winston Churchill, Princess Diana, Ben Stiller, Al Pacino and John Kirwan, just to name a few.

Over the years I have altered the way I look at and talk about the illness. Nowadays I have the attitude of, 'If it's good enough for them, well it's good enough for me. If Isaac Newton had it, why shouldn't I?' The trick is to look at it with a different mindset. Rather than say to myself, 'Why me?' I say, 'Why not me?'

Thankfully, the stigma associated with depression and other mental illnesses has lessened in recent years due to better education about the condition and more sufferers being willing to speak out. However, I think there's still a lot to be done before depression is looked upon in the same way as physical illnesses such as asthma, diabetes and arthritis. There is still a tendency for non-sufferers to regard depression as not being a 'proper' illness, but merely a condition that the sufferer should make the effort to simply 'snap out' of. I can tell you from personal experience that you can't 'snap out' of depression any more than you can 'snap out' of asthma, diabetes or arthritis, and remember, telling someone not to be depressed is as futile as telling someone not to have cancer.

I'm well now. I may not get another bout as long as I'm on God's earth, but my understanding of depression is such that I realise I could succumb to it again: who knows? The one thing I do know however, is that if it were to come knocking at my door again, I'm far more knowledgeable and better equipped mentally to handle it. I won't have any fear of asking for help. Society is much more accepting of people with depression and sufferers need not be wary of confiding in their friends and families.

People often say that when 'fighting' depression, they tell themselves, 'Come on, you can do it. You can beat it.' As if it's a condition you can eradicate and be 'cured' of. When I hear this being said my response is to comment that, from my experience, that mindset is not 'fighting' depression, it's making yourself more anxious. To me, after all these years of suffering the utter despair of the illness, the best way of 'fighting' depression is 'accepting' it. Once you accept that you have the illness, or are susceptible to suffering from it, you can still live life fully but within the context and confines of the condition.

The analogy I use is, if a rugby player pulls a hamstring they have to stop playing or even training for a while, but they could jog a few laps, lift some weights or do some cycling. In other words, they can train within the confines of the injury until they are fully fit and playing again. It's the same with depression. It is about accepting it and trying to live with it instead of mentally trying to battle against it twenty-four hours a day.

Mind you, it's taken me almost 30 years to come to that conclusion, 30 years of anxiety and frustration to finally understand and appreciate it. In the past, when a bout of depression came on, I would be of the 'Oh no, not again!' mindset, which serves only to feed the illness' evil twin – anxiety. Then I'd be back on the rollercoaster ride which I couldn't get off.

Now I accept that I have a susceptibility to depression and I'm relaxed about it. I'm open with it. It's part of who I am. I'm not boasting about it, but I'm not hiding it either.

I'm Phil Steele and I suffer with depression – but I'm still here, and I'm still me.

Note from Anthony Bunko

From the very first day we met up it's been an absolute pleasure to work with Phil on Nerves of Steele. He is a true gentleman, a complete professional and even on the occasions when we have delved into some very sad events in his life, he's always done it with style and, where appropriate, a sense of humour.

I always find it such an honour and privilege when a person I respect allows me to not only enter into their life, but trusts me enough to write their life story for publication. So, I'd like to thank Phil – who I now class as a good mate – for giving me that opportunity.

Lots of love to you and your family.

Stay Free Phil!

Bunko x